THE HIJACKING

OF

AMERICAN EDUCATION

From Little Black Sambo

to

Critical Race Theory

ROBERT V. CARABINA

Contents

Preface   ix

1. The Early Years   1

    School "Daze"   1

    School Prayer and Pledge of Allegiance   5

    The Story of Little Black Sambo   6

    "Jethro Bodine" School of Promotion-Retention   7

    Duck and Cover: The Russians are Coming   9

    Polio Pandemic   11

    Captain of the Rifle Team   13

    "Old Math" vs. "New Math"   14

    Vietnam War   16

2. College Years   23

    Broken Vows   23

    Undercover Bob   24

    Hong Kong Flu vs. Covid-19   35

3. A New Beginning   39

    The Death of Little Black Sambo   39

    How Schools Manipulate Student Records   40

Old School vs. New School   42

Taxpayers are Robbed   44

Love at First Sight   45

To Be or Not To Be: Career Assessment   50

The Baby Jesus Under Attack   52

Mary Jane and Her Cousin Cocaine   54

4.   Suffer Little Children   59

Small School Building, Small Problems; Big School Building, Big Problems   59

The Big Cover-Up or It's Snowing in the Classroom   60

Polluted Drinking Water or Water So Toxic That Nemo and Dory Would Not Survive   65

Sins of the Church – Bad Clergy Men   67

The Sinners   67

The Enablers   69

A Good Idea Gone Bad – Shut Down This Building   71

Retaliation and Racism: Enter "The Hatchet Man" and "Attila the Nun"   72

Big Brother   75

University Bound   79

5. Attempts to Fix Our Schools   81

    "Just Say No to Drugs"   81

    Saying No to Drugs is Easier Said Than Done   83

    Legalization of Marijuana   90

    Recertification of Teachers   91

    No Child Left Behind   102

    Assault on Standardized Testing   103

6. Where has Civics Instruction Gone?   107

    Diary of Anne Frank   108

    Jewish Holocaust   112

    Censorship   114

    Civics Instruction vs. Holocaust Studies   115

    Other Victims of Atrocities   117

    Black History   120

    Say Our Name   121

    What Dat?   122

    LGBTQ   123

    Old Glory vs. LGBTQ Banner   131

    Anti-Bullying Rules   132

    Demise of Civics Instruction   133

7. Cancel Culture   135

    War on American Values   135

    National Symbols of the United States   138

    The Flag and The Star-Spangled Banner   143

    1776 or 1619   153

    Thanksgiving Day   159

    Andy Jackson or Auntie   162

    Mount Rushmore   163

    Juneteenth   164

    Teddy Roosevelt   165

    Christopher Columbus   168

    Freemasons and American Values   175

    It's Time to Cancel "Cancel Culture"   179

8. Critical Race Theory   183

    White Devils   183

    African Chiefs Enabled the Slave Trade   189

    Critical Race Theory Invades the Military   191

    Radicals at the Federal Reserve Banks   193

    *Debt Forgiveness for Black Farmers and
    Ranchers*   199

    "40 Acres and a Mule" in the 21st Century   200

Department of Defense vs. State Department   206

Special Instructions for White People   208

Juneteenth or "Jubilee Day"   209

Destruction of America's Pastime   214

From Little Black Sambo to Black Lives Matter   217

Opposition to Critical Race Theory   232

Just Say "No!"   236

9. Black Criminals White Victims   239

Figures Don't Lie But Liars Figure   239

The "Combat Zone"   241

Mayhem in the Graveyard   245

Nursing Home Tragedy   246

Five-Year-Old Shot Dead   248

Four-Year-Old Boy Abducted and Murdered   249

Death at Dunkin' Donuts   251

Macy's Beat Down   253

Hail Caesar   254

Whitey in the Crosshairs   255

Granny Woke   256

Restaurant Face-Off   260

High on Mushrooms, Short on Brains   263

Reeducation of White Women   264

*Better to be Judged by Twelve Than
Carried by Six*   267

*How the Failure to Call 911 Led to a Young
Woman's Death*   275

The Sad Case of George Floyd   277

10. At a Crossroads: The Future of Education   289

Preface

"The only thing necessary for the *triumph of evil* is for good men to do nothing."

That quote has been attributed to Edmund Burke, an eighteenth-century Irish philosopher and statesman. There is no evidence, however, that Burke ever said those words. One thing is certain though, whomever uttered that quote, must have had a keen understanding of the age-old conflict between good and evil in society. Nowhere was that conflict more apparent than in the U.S. during 2020-2021.

Those years will be known in history for the Covid-19 pandemic. In the U.S., that period also represents a time of social upheaval and unrest. Cities have been burned to the ground by unruly mobs representing Black Lives Matter (BLM) and Antifa while politicians in those cities have turned a blind eye to the carnage. Moreover, there has been a concerted effort by groups who have threatened to upend our cherished institutions and national heritage. Their intention is to cancel our culture and rewrite our nation's history. In addition, they have fervently avowed to take no prisoners.

Furthermore, our nation's schools have come under unrelenting

attack by the cancel culture protagonists who wish to replace

our core educational curriculum and values with "critical race

theory".

In addition, we have witnessed an unparalleled

censorship of free speech never before experienced in our

nation's history. The censors stretch across all mediums,

including social media, print media, and telecommunications.

Censorship also abounds in education, sports, our armed

forces, corporate enterprises, and government agencies. For

those who have disobeyed the "book burners" the punishment

has included loss of employment, financial ruin, character

assassination, and reeducation classes. In addition, social media

has gone to great lengths to suppress free thought. It has

removed accounts of persons whose views are not in agreement

with its prevailing propaganda and lies. Is this the society we

once knew or is it something from the novel, *1984*?

Not surprisingly, there is no longer two sides to an

issue. An NBC news anchor, for example, declared that

fairness was overrated in reporting the news. He added that it was not necessary to give advocates of both sides of an issue an equal opportunity to express their views. Furthermore, a writer at *New York Time Magazine* has applauded journalists who are activists. Since when has the advancement of a questionable set of beliefs founded on lies been considered journalism? Excuse me, but there *are* two sides to an issue.

As part of the effort to undermine our nation's schools, popular children's books such as *The Story of Little Black Sambo* and those written under the name of Dr. Seuss have been blacklisted in our nation's schools. Additionally, the works of Mark Twain and William Shakespeare have been deemed verboten by those who espouse the doctrine of critical race theory on the pretext that those classic writings promote systemic racism. Who suffers the most from the actions of those who wish to cancel our culture and replace it with critical race theory propaganda? The children who attend our nation's schools are the unsuspecting victims of those lies.

In order to present a more balanced account of the upheaval that has taken place in our nation's schools, I have decided to take pen to paper and write this book. It covers the years 1949-2021 and offers a presentation of the events that have played a role in the transformation of our schools during that period. The events on which I have reported focus on the radical changes undergone in our public schools that have taken us from teaching the fundamentals to the teaching of its twin adversaries, namely cancel culture and critical race theory. My experiences as a student and an educator allow me to provide a firsthand account of those changes that have undermined our educational system. There is no doubt that the protagonists of cancel culture and critical race theory are determined to permanently transform our schools.

Furthermore, as a witness to the social unrest, destruction of our national monuments, riots, looting, and murder that have plagued our nation, I am providing this unbiased account of the tumultuous events of 2020-2021. Fair and balanced reporting is required if future generations are to form a critical assessment of our times. Unlike the journalists who perceive themselves as political activists, I do believe there are two sides to every story.

The events I describe in this book are supported by facts and research. Moreover, anecdotal accounts of my firsthand experiences and observations are presented to keep the reader engaged in the narrative. I pull no punches. Consider my writing an uncensored account of the events of the day. It is a must read for anybody who detests censorship and propaganda.

Bob Carabina

Chapter One

The Early Years

1. School "Daze"

It was 1949. Harry Truman was president of the U.S. following his stunning victory over Thomas Dewey in the 1948 presidential election. The Bronx Bombers of New York, the incomparable New York Yankees, would go on to win another World Series. The price of regular leaded gasoline was $0.27 a gallon. Yes, you read that correctly. Leaded gasoline powered vehicles in the U.S. in 1949. Unleaded gas was not made available until the 1970s. In addition, American workers celebrated an increase in their paychecks. The minimum wage was dramatically increased from $0.40 to $0.75 an hour. And bravely, I had entered first grade. It was my first year of school. In 1949, there was no pre-school for children. Similarly, there was no kindergarten. School began in first grade. Heaven forbid!

On my first day of school, I was still four years old.

Notwithstanding the fact that I could recite the alphabet, print my name, and perform some basic arithmetic operations, the principal believed that I was too young to be starting school. She suggested that I return the following year. My mother, however, held the opposite opinion. Therefore, an agreement between my mother and the principal was reached to resolve the impasse. It allowed me to attend school for a trial period of two weeks to see how I would perform in class. At the end of two weeks, a reassessment would be made to determine my standing in class.

Things were moving along without incident during those first two weeks. Socially, I had begun to develop friendships with other classmates. In addition, I had no problems completing the class assignments. Then one day my teacher, Ms. McGovern, lost her composure in the classroom. She was a female curmudgeon nearing the age of mandatory retirement which in teaching would have been approximately seventy-two. Why she was still teaching first graders defied comprehension. On this day, she was instructing the class on the recitation of the alphabet. As she called on my classmates,

2

student after student failed in their attempts at reciting the alphabet. Nobody could recite it beyond the middle of the alphabet. That was the last straw for the teacher. Angrily, she opened her desk drawer and withdrew a formidable looking instrument of punishment made from oak. Forcefully, she slammed that "stick" onto her desk. Ms. McGovern then threatened the class with physical punishment. She warned us that if the next person she called on to recite the letters of the alphabet was unable to do so, that individual would receive a thorough beating with the stick. Guess who was called upon to recite the alphabet? Like a spider calling a fly, Ms. McGovern selected me to recite the letters of the alphabet. Shakingly, I proceeded to stand up and stood there trying to recite the alphabet. My mind was processing the list of letters - a, b, c, d, and so on - but my vocal cords produced no sound. As I looked down on the wooden floor of the classroom, I could see the beads of perspiration that had fallen from my forehead onto the floor. Although I knew the alphabet, I was paralyzed with fear and could not speak the letters. It was as though I had been struck by lightning. Ms. McGovern, seeing that I was visibly shaken, told me to sit down and pay attention. That ended my first year in school. My mother was furious over the conduct of Ms. McGovern, who emphatically denied any wrongdoing in the matter. Both the principal and Ms. McGovern had insisted, however, that I should wait until the following year to return to school when I would be at a higher level of maturity.

That was school life in the first grade during the middle of the twentieth century. The teachers were relics of a bygone era. It was my misfortune to have a seventy-year-old lady, who was lacking in patience and ruling with a wooden paddle, as my first grade teacher. In today's public schools, there would be no place of employment for such a person.

Had I remained in school that first year, I would have graduated from high school at sixteen instead of seventeen. Fortunately, my brother Jim, who is three years my junior, did not have to endure an entire school year of Ms. McGovern. She had retired just before he had started school. Unlike me, Jim began school in kindergarten. His teachers in grade school were freshly-minted, twenty-something-year-olds who brought with them a great deal of patience and energy. Lucky guy!

2. School Prayer and Pledge of Allegiance

It was customary to begin school days with the Lord's Prayer and a recitation of the Pledge of Allegiance. What could be wrong with those opening exercises? Well, leave it to the godless souls to protest the Lord's Prayer by filing a lawsuit and taking it all the way up to the U.S. Supreme Court. As you may have expected, the U.S. Supreme Court banned school-sponsored prayer in public schools in a 1962 decision, stating that it violated the First Amendment.

Whose rights were violated under the First Amendment? The godless socialists who to this day want to undermine our entire public school system! And what about the First Amendment rights of those who wished to begin the school day with a thoughtful prayer? Shame on the Court for their decision.

3. The Story of Little Black Sambo

This image is in the public domain. Its illustrator was Florence White Williams. Williams died in 1953.

My favorite first-grade reader was *The Story of Little Black Sambo*. It is a book for children written and illustrated by Helen Bannerman, a Scottish author, which was published in 1899. I still remember the main characters from the story. They were Little Black Sambo; his father, Black Jumbo; and his mother, Black Mumbo. And then there were the tigers.

In the climax to the story, the tigers furiously chased each other around a tree trying to eat each other. They whirled around so fast that they appeared as a blur to the naked eye. Faster and faster they ran until they just melted away. Nothing of their existence remained except a pool of melted butter.

Happily, Little Black Sambo collected the butter in a bucket and brought it home to his mother. Black Mumbo then proceeded to whip up some pancakes for the family and generously topped them off with the fresh butter, courtesy of the tigers.

That story was a favorite of children for over a half century. It found its way into the curriculum of our public schools at the turn of the twentieth century and was a mainstay for decades. Predictably, the book was criticized as being racist and it can no longer be found in a first-grade classroom in the public schools of the U.S.

4. "Jethro Bodine" School of Promotion-Retention

In order to "pass" from one grade level to the next grade level during the years I had attended public school, a student needed to demonstrate a certain level of proficiency in reading, writing, and arithmetic. In education, it was known as the "3 Rs". If a student failed those primary subjects, he or she would be retained at the same grade level and repeat the year.

It was quite common to find sixteen-year-olds in the sixth grade in this system of pass-fail. I refer to it as the "Jethro Bodine" system of promotion-retention. In the "Beverly Hillbillies" television series of the 1960s, one of the show's characters, Jethro, proudly announced that he had graduated from school with a fourth grade education.

Not surprisingly, by the time I had reached sixth-grade, I found myself in a classroom that consisted of at least a half-dozen "Jethros", male and female. The rule then was that a student could "quit" school at the age of sixteen. To nobody's surprise, the exodus from my classroom was in full swing that year. I can't really fault those students from leaving school. Would anybody want to continue in grade-school at the age of sixteen surrounded by classmates as young as eleven? I think not.

At some point, the "masterminds" who ran our public schools, saw the flaw in a system of promotion-retention which doomed young adults to hopelessness and created social incompatibility among students who ranged in age from eleven to sixteen. Thus, began the era of "social" promotion which is still with us today. Under "social" promotion, nobody failed and thus were not subject to retention. It didn't matter if a child lacked the basic skills of reading, writing, and arithmetic. He or she just moved on to the next grade level.

5. Duck and Cover: The Russians are Coming

During the 1950s, schools across the U.S. were training students to hide under their desks and cover their heads. It was referred to as "duck and cover" drills and were intended for our safety in the event of a nuclear attack by the Soviet Union. Yeah, that would have worked really well if an atomic bomb had landed in my school yard. More likely, we would have been blown to smithereens along with our desks and the entire school building. Since I had lived in the Northeast, my elementary school had a basement in which we would gather to practice duck and cover drills instead of hiding under our desks. Presumably, the thinking was, by assembling in the basement of the building we were afforded slightly more protection than remaining in our classrooms which were above street level.

What were the events that had led to the Soviet Union becoming a nuclear threat to world peace? By the time I had entered first grade, the U.S. had been the only nation on the planet which had possessed nuclear weapons. However, that was to change, courtesy of Julius and Ethel Rosenberg. Julius was born in New York City to Jewish parents who had emigrated from Russia. Ethel was also born to a Jewish family in New York City. Both Julius and Ethel were, at times in their lives, members of Communist organizations. The couple was accused of spying and providing classified information about nuclear weapon designs along with other top secret information to the Soviets. They were convicted of espionage and sentenced to death. The Rosenbergs died in June 1953, strapped to the electric chair, in the Sing Sing correctional facility in New York. Needless to say, they and their followers received quite a shock on the day of their demise.

The espionage activities by the Rosenbergs enabled the Soviets to become the second major world power to possess nuclear weapons. This plunged the U.S. and the Soviet Union

10

into a cold war punctuated by a nuclear arms race. It also plunged the world into a gripping fear of nuclear annihilation.

6. Polio Pandemic

During the late 1940s and into the 1950s, one of the most feared diseases in the U.S. was polio. Polio was a disabling disease, causing paralysis in individuals. Parents were frightened to let their children go outside and play with their friends. Moreover, travel was regulated in many areas, including restrictions which were placed on commerce between affected cities. Additionally, public health officials imposed quarantines on residential dwellings and on entire towns in which its occupants had been diagnosed with cases of polio.

During that time, I had lived in an apartment building with my family. There are recollections that I still have of buildings that had signs that read, "Quarantine" and "Keep Out". No more than five or six-years-old, I remember asking my mother what was that large word on the sign that began with the letter "Q". She explained, "Quarantine". I implored, "What does that mean." Again, she patiently explained, "It means that there are some very sick people in that building. So don't go there".

Eventually, vaccines were developed to combat the disease. One vaccine was developed by Jonas Salk and was given by injection. A second vaccine, given orally, was developed by Albert Sabin.

School children began receiving injections of the polio vaccine in early 1954. Medical staff visited my elementary school and gave us the vaccine injections. We bravely lined up to receive our shots, except for one boy. William was his name, and he was stationed immediately in front of me in that lengthy line. He wanted absolutely nothing to do with the shot. The medical staff, however, did not have the time or patience for gentle persuasion. Poor William was led kicking and screaming into the nurses station to receive his inoculation. Henceforth, William was known to his classmates as Willie.

The polio vaccine was an enormous success. Since 1979, no cases of polio have *originated* in the U.S. The virus that causes polio, however, has been brought into the U.S. by *travelers*. The last time that had occurred was in 1993.

7. Captain of the Rifle Team

In the eighth grade, I had joined the rifle team. It didn't take me long to advance to the level of sharpshooter and I had been named captain of the rifle squad. We competed against other rifle teams in the Northeast with notable success. My coach was an ex-Army service member named George D'Espard Fawcett III. In his spare time, George was engaged in the study of UFOs. George shared with us many stories of UFOs told to him by pilots he had known from his time in the military. He told us that the military had a gag order on the subject and had forbidden pilots to publicly disclose sightings they may have encountered during their flights.

Many years later, as I was travelling in my auto and listening to a talk show about UFOs, the host of the program identified his guest as George Fawcett, one of the nation's leading experts on UFOs. I recognized the voice and I knew it was my former coach of the rifle team. With a little luck and determination, I was able to locate the whereabouts of George and had gotten his telephone number. Unsure if he would remember me some thirty years later, I called him at his home.

Indeed, George remembered me and we had a long chat. I

extended my congratulations to him for his recognition by the

science community as an expert on UFOs. George inquired if I

was still active in shooting competition. I explained I still

enjoyed the sport and continued to shoot as a hobby. George

complimented me as being one of the finest marksmen he had

the privilege of coaching over the years.

8. "Old Math" vs. "New Math"

The eighth grade was a turning point for students in the

U.S. in 1957. The math curriculum was about to undergo a

massive overhaul, courtesy of the Soviet Union. On October 4,

1957, the Soviet Union launched the earth's first artificial

satellite, Sputnik I. In doing so, it allowed the Soviets to gain a

head start on the U.S. in the space race.

Our leaders were appalled at the prospect of the Soviets

being first in space. In consultation with academia and the

science community, our government decided it was necessary

to make some radical changes in our school curriculum. Most

notably, it was decided that both the math and science curricula would undergo massive revision. It was hoped that this would enable our educational institutions to provide the nation with the best minds in the fields of math and science, thereby allowing us to compete with the Soviets for preeminence in the space race.

One day, a rather dapper looking gentleman came to my school and spoke to my math class about something he called "new math". For our purposes we will refer to him as Dapper Dan. Dapper was from the R.I. Board of Education. What he had to tell us intrigued the class. According to Dapper Dan, the math curriculum was going to undergo a radical overhaul. Putting it succinctly, it was "out with the old and in with the new". That made us groan at the thought of relearning math. Did we want to undertake learning "new math" after spending years learning what was now considered "old math"? No!

The groans, however, soon turned into cheers. Dapper assured us that we would not be learning "new math". Instead, we would continue with "old math" throughout the remaining years of our public school education. He went on to elaborate that we were the cutoff class for the transition from "old math" to "new math". He added that, upon graduation from high school, we would be the last class to have studied "old math". Henceforth, it would be the students who had graduated from high school after 1962, who would be the recipients of instruction in the "new math" curriculum.

9. Vietnam War

Say what? That's the question students in my U.S. History class in 1961 asked, when the news had surfaced that the U.S. may be facing a ten-year long conflict in Southeast Asia in a country called Vietnam.

As the top student in my U.S. History class, I was a news junkie and enthusiastically watched the evening news on a regular basis. The Huntley-Brinkley Report that had aired on NBC from 1956-1970 was my favorite evening newscast. Chet Huntley, who was reporting from New York City, and David Brinkley, who was reporting from Washington, DC, were the anchors for the news program. When I was in college, I had the opportunity to meet David Brinkley at a symposium that featured a discussion of current events including the Vietnam War.

One evening in the spring of 1961, as I had watched the evening news, I recall Huntley and Brinkley having reported that our Secretary of Defense, Robert S. McNamara, had just returned from a visit to Southeast Asia. McNamara had issued a dire report that the U.S. must be prepared for a protracted conflict in Southeast Asia. He warned that we were facing a ten-year war in Vietnam.

The next day in class, it was my turn to report on the news of the day (actually the prior day). So, I broached the topic of a ten-year conflict in Vietnam. Our teacher instructed one of my classmates to unfurl the map of the world, which was hanging above the blackboard (is it politically correct to say that) and locate Vietnam. A little effort led us to a rather tiny speck called Vietnam tucked away in Southeast Asia on the world map.

My classmates had burst out in haughty laughter. We had dismissed the notion that a small land mass such as Vietnam could command a ten-year conflict. Comments were offered by classmates that we (U.S.) would run amok over Vietnam in weeks, thereby bringing any war to a speedy and victorious conclusion.

My teacher, who was an avowed Democrat and an influential member of the local Democrat City Committee, cautioned us against being dismissive of the current administration's plans for Southeast Asia. Especially a war in Vietnam, which was the focus of our discussion. I remember her having stated with absolute finality, "If President Kennedy says we will be engaged in a ten-year war, then we will be engaged in a ten-year war."

Arguably, Robert S. McNamara is considered to have been the architect of the Vietnam War. McNamara had served as secretary of defense from 1961-1968 under Presidents John F. Kennedy and Lyndon B. Johnson. According to Kennedy apologists, had John F. Kennedy not been assassinated and had completed his presidency, he would have kept the U.S. out of a prolonged conflict in Vietnam. Don't ever believe it! If Kennedy were truly in opposition to a conflict in Vietnam, he would have replaced Robert S. McNamara as his secretary of defense early in his administration.

Late in his life, McNamara had written that he was at odds with President Johnson over the war and he had wanted the U.S. to withdraw from the conflict. This contention is without merit. His claim is false! It is another example of a policymaker refusing to accept responsibility for his own actions. Robert S. McNamara, born Robert Strange McNamara, could not have been more appropriately named by his parents.

How long was the war in Vietnam? There is conflicting data on the length of time of the war in Vietnam. I have read news articles and have seen documentaries that have claimed the war lasted anywhere from a minimum of eight years to a maximum of twenty years. Why is there such a lack of agreement on the length of the war? The lack of agreement stems from the fact that some accounts of the war consider its beginning to include the years when the U.S. had initially sent military advisers to South Vietnam. On the other hand, others recognize the attack on U.S. vessels by North Vietnamese torpedo boats in the Gulf of Tonkin in 1964 as the official commencement of the war. The Gulf of Tonkin Resolution was passed by Congress on August 7, 1964[1] and authorized President Lyndon Johnson to "take all necessary measures to repel any armed attack against the forces of the United States and to prevent further aggression"[2] by the North Vietnam Communist government.

There is more consensus on the end of the Vietnam War than there is on the beginning of the war. On January 27, 1973, President Richard Nixon signed the Paris Peace Accords, thereby ending direct U.S. involvement in the Vietnam War. In the spring of 1975, the last remaining Americans still in South Vietnam were airlifted out of the country as it fell to North Vietnamese Communist forces.

How many Americans died in service in Vietnam? The Vietnam Veterans Memorial Wall in Washington, DC, which was dedicated on November 10, 1982, includes a total of

[1] History.com Editors. (2019, June 7 updated). *Gulf of Tonkin Resolution*. History. Retrieved October 17, 2021, from http://www.history.com/topics/vietnam-war/gulf-of-tonkin-resolution-1
[2] Ibid.

58,318[3] names listed on it as of Memorial Day 2017. It includes those who remain missing-in-action.

[3] Veterans of Foreign Wars. (2017, November 13). *Vietnam Memorial Turns 35*. Retrieved October 16, 2021, from https://www.vfw.org/media-and-events/latest-releases/archives/2017/11/vietnam-veterans-memorial-turns-35

Chapter Two

College Years

1. Broken Vows

Providence College (PC) was my alma mater. It is a Catholic college located in the now sanctuary city of Providence, RI. PC is well-known for its successful basketball program and competes in the Big East Conference. In general, Catholic schools are run either by the Dominican or the Jesuit religious orders of the Catholic Church. The Dominican Friars have the honor of being the gatekeepers at PC. Hence, the school's nickname is the Providence College Friars. During the years of my attendance, it was an all-male school. In 1970, however, the college decided to admit women and became a co-ed institution commencing with the 1971-1972 academic year. Welcome to the twentieth century, Friars.

The President of the college during my days at PC was a Dominican priest. His official title was Rev. William Paul Haas, O.P. Father Haas had a reputation of being an elusive soul. He was not readily accessible to the students at the

23

college and there were persistent rumors that he was playing "hide the salami" with his secretary. In the case of Haas, the rumors proved true. Short of taking a cyanide capsule, he did the next best thing and resigned as President of the college. Subsequently, he severed all connections to PC and resigned from his faculty position at the school. In 1973, Pope Paul VI granted him a dispensation from his priestly obligations which allowed him the right to marry. Shortly thereafter, he was laicized and married his former secretary. Although he had broken his vows, there is one redeeming quality that may be said about the "good" father. Haas may have run off with his secretary; at least he didn't run off with the altar boy.

2. Undercover Bob

In 1968, I had graduated from college. It was a year of tumultuous events.

The nation bore witness to the assassinations of Martin Luther King on April 4, 1968 and that of Robert F. Kennedy just two months later on June 6, 1968. Furthermore, there were protests against the Vietnam War in cities and on college campuses throughout the U. S. Protesters expressed their displeasure at the number of deaths and casualties suffered by American armed forces in Vietnam. President Lyndon Baines Johnson (LBJ) was under scathing attack for the manner in which the war was being conducted by the bureaucrats in Washington, DC. Protesters hurled epithets such as, "LBJ! LBJ! How many boys have you killed today?" Finally, Johnson succumbed to the mounting pressure and declined to run for re-election.

Vice-President Hubert Humphrey was nominated at the Democrat Convention as its standard bearer. Former vice-president and unsuccessful candidate for the presidency in 1960, Richard M. Nixon, was the nominee of the Republican Party. The American Independent Party nominated the Democrat Governor of Alabama, George C. Wallace. After all votes had been counted, Nixon emerged victorious garnering 301 electoral votes to Humphrey's 191 votes and Wallace's 46 votes.

In addition, the emergence of the Hong Kong Flu, would leave its mark on the world's population. The flu was caused by the influenza A (H3N2) virus, which had originated in China. The ensuing pandemic ran its course of sickness and death from 1968 - 1969. At the time, it had the notoriety of being the third influenza pandemic of the 20th century. The Hong Kong Flu had been preceded by the Asian Flu of 1957-1958 and the Spanish Flu of 1918-1919.

Notwithstanding the upheavals of 1968, it was a time for college graduates to seek employment in the workforce. I had wanted to pursue a career in federal law enforcement and had arranged for several interviews with various federal agencies. Illegal drugs were of paramount concern to the government. In order to combat the smuggling of illicit drugs into the U.S., various federal agencies were seeking new hires to work undercover and infiltrate the drug-dealing networks.

Scheduling an interview was not a problem. Getting into the interviewer's office was a challenge. Anti-war protests were rampant nationwide. Protesters targeted government agencies that were interviewing college graduates. One of their tactics would be to lie down in front of the interviewer's office to obstruct anybody going into the office for an interview. In my case, I literally had to step over (and sometimes step on) those protesters as I made my way to the interview room.

There were three noteworthy federal agencies who were recruiting potential hires. One was the Federal Bureau of Investigation (FBI). The FBI, however, was still under the leadership of J. Edgar Hoover. Hoover was primarily recruiting attorneys and accountants for positions within the agency. In other words, he was looking to hire "suits". After having led the FBI for forty-eight years, Hoover died in 1972. It was at that time, that the FBI began to undergo changes in its hiring practices. In 1968, however, Hoover continued to exert extreme influence within the agency.

Two, the Health Department was another agency that was interested in recruits. The agency was embarking upon a program to eradicate syphilis in the U.S. The objective was to hire recruits to work undercover in the larger cities. Agents would live among people of dubious character and encourage them to seek treatment for their disease.

Three, there was the U.S. Customs Service. It had three major missions. First, collecting tariff revenue. Second, protecting the U.S. from smuggling operations and illegal

goods which threatened our economy. Third, processing people

and goods at ports of entry. Customs was interested in hiring

me to work undercover in its drive to combat smugglers and

illegal goods from entering the U.S. It was an extremely high-

risk job and involved long hours of surveillance. If the FBI was

a "gentlemen's club" for "suits", then Customs was a "blue

collar", "get in your face" type of hazardous endeavor. In

addition, Customs had enormous law enforcement powers,

even exceeding those of the FBI.

Nothing, however, lasts forever. The U.S. Customs

Service, formed in 1789, ceased operations as an independent

agency of the U.S. federal government in 2003. After the

terrorist attacks on September 11, 2001 (9/11), it was

reorganized under Homeland Security and renamed the Bureau

of Customs and Border Protection.

My interview with the U.S. Customs Service went well

and I was offered a position as a field agent. Translation:

undercover work. The life expectancy of a field agent was

short. I was told that after five years in the field, I would be promoted to a supervisory position. I asked the recruiter to elaborate on that promise. He said that one of three things would happen within that five-year period. One, I would resign from the agency. Two, I would be killed in the line of duty. Three, I would be promoted from field agent to supervisor. Furthermore, I would be given an alias. In the event of my death, the agency would disavow any knowledge of my employment.

The actual work of a government undercover agent is not what Hollywood portrays in its movies. There is no glitz and glitter that comes with the job. And there is definitely no supermodel waiting for you at the end of your assignment.

My tenure at Customs, however, was derailed by the Hong Kong Flu. It was a devastating experience. The doctors didn't know how to deal with this version of the flu or virus. Antibiotics did not work because the version of the flu I had contracted was viral and not bacterial in nature. My symptoms were a persistent and uncontrollable cough. Moreover, the virus invaded my trachea (breathing tube or windpipe). That was not good. The medical terminology was viral tracheitis.

Whenever I had coughed, my windpipe would spasm and I would collapse for lack of oxygen. It was like being a victim of strangulation or drowning. The doctors placed me in a hospital, and I was given oxygen. They also discussed the possibility of a tracheotomy to open up my airways. Additionally, I was given the last rites by a local parish priest. As a last resort, the doctors recommended steroid drugs which mitigated my symptoms. Fortunately, I was able to avoid a tracheotomy.

During that period of time, I had to restrict my activities especially those which required physical exertion. Just walking up a flight of stairs was a challenge. Therefore, I took an indefinite leave of absence from Customs. There was no way of knowing just how long it would take me to fully recover from the complications of the virus.

Moreover, because of side effects from the prolonged use of the medication, my doctor discontinued its treatment and referred me to a specialist for an alternative treatment plan. It took approximately four years from the onset of the flu (virus) and subsequent medical treatments before I could fully regain my ability to engage in strenuous physical activities.

Not until the pandemic of 2020-2021, did I realize how ill I truly was in 1968 from the Hong Kong Flu. My empathies are with the victims and their families who have suffered the effects from Covid-19. It is my honest opinion, that the doctors of today know little more about Covid-19 than their counterparts did in 1968 about the Hong Kong Flu.

Whatever benefits I had been entitled to had been exhausted due to the short period of time that I had been employed by Customs. Therefore, I spoke to my supervisor and informed him of my intent to seek temporary employment elsewhere that involved less strenuous activity. Once fully recovered, I would petition for reinstatement to my former duties as an agent. He agreed with my decision. He added that his door and that of the agency's would be open to my returning to work, whenever I had fully regained my health. Thus, I embarked upon a job search for a position that would allow me to be gainfully employed and at the same time continue my recovery.

Most of the job postings that I had reviewed, however, would have required varying degrees of physical exertion;

others did not pique my interest. Therefore, I called a friend and asked his advice on potential job offerings. He suggested that I consider a teaching position. I told him that I did not have a certificate in education. In addition, it was late summer and schools were about to open in a week. He advised me to go "knock on doors" in some of the smaller towns in the area. The smaller towns, he added, were always the last ones to fill their teaching positions. To that end, I decided to give it a try and see if I could obtain employment in education as a teacher.

It is said that the third time is a charm. After being told in two of the towns I had visited that their teaching positions for the new academic year had been filled, I was offered a position in the town of Bellingham, Massachusetts, the third stop in my job pursuit. I walked into the superintendent of school's office and was given an interview on the spot. I had no resume on hand. The superintendent and I commenced speaking for about half an hour. He told me that although I did not have any teaching credentials, I did have something that other applicants did not have and that was *charisma*. He said that he would hire me on a conditional basis. The condition

32

being that I would have to enroll in education classes to satisfy

the state requirements for certification in the public schools. I

agreed to his terms.

He added that the town's public schools were suffering

from overcrowded conditions. It was so bad that the sixth and

seventh grades would be in "double sessions" in one of the

town's school buildings. The sixth-grade students would

occupy the building in the morning session, from 8:00 - 12:30,

and the seventh-grade students would be assigned to the

afternoon session, from 1:00 - 5:30. He had one position to fill

and asked me to choose between the sixth-grade morning

session and the seventh-grade afternoon session. I chose the

morning session which I believed to be the better choice since I

was an early riser.

Actually, it was a no-brainer. Four and one-half hours a

day, five days a week, vacations, and summers off at full

salary. In addition, my salary was $300 higher than the starting

salary at Customs. More importantly, it gave me the time I had

needed to continue treatment to recover from the effects of the

virus.

So, where is Bellingham, Massachusetts? What are its qualities of life? Bellingham sits on the southwestern edge of Metropolitan Boston along the growing beltway that is Route 495. Incorporated in 1719, it still retained vestiges of its earlier years as a predominantly rural community when the horse and buggy were the major means of transportation, and one schoolhouse provided the education for the children of the entire town. Lacking any major industry of its own or a robust job base, its signature characteristic was that of a middle-class, suburban, bedroom community. It was the type of community in which someone could find comfort if they were a fugitive from justice or perhaps just recovering from a major illness.

Moreover, Bellingham, along with its neighbors, Blackstone, Massachusetts, and Woonsocket, Rhode Island were considered a culturally depressed area in 1968. According to government census data, those towns, collectively, ranked lower than Appalachia with regards to their lack of cultural growth. And that is pretty low.

3. Hong Kong Flu vs. Covid-19

According to the Centers for Disease Control and Prevention (CDC), the Hong Kong Flu that gave rise to the pandemic of 1968-1969 was caused by the influenza A (H3N2) virus. The estimated number of deaths worldwide were one million. There have been other accounts, however, that have pegged the estimated number of deaths at between one to four million. The number of deaths in the U.S. was estimated at 100,000. Moreover, most deaths had been recorded in persons 65 years and older. Furthermore, the virus has been very resourceful and continues to circulate worldwide as a seasonal influenza A virus. It is called the flu but it could just as easily be referred to as a virus. And it is the reason that we are encouraged by health care professionals to receive an annual flu shot.

The Coronavirus or Covid-19 is the latest pandemic. It is alleged to have begun in 2020 (as early as 2019 according to some accounts) and continues to wreak havoc worldwide as of this writing. Not surprisingly, the virus has mutated and created a surge in new cases as we near the end of 2021. Where it goes from here is anybody's guess. The pandemic has become a political football and was weaponized to oust former President Donald Trump from office in the 2020 Presidential election. Moreover, the American public have now lost faith in the new administration of President Joseph Biden. Additionally, contradicting information from both the medical and science communities has shaken the trust of the American people.

As I had written earlier, Covid-19 has helped me understand the influenza A virus which had struck me down in 1968. The influenza A virus was never scrutinized by the media pundits. Nor was it given ample news coverage. That was due in part to the preoccupation with the assassinations of Martin Luther King and Robert F. Kennedy. In addition, momentum had been growing in opposition to the Vietnam War, replete with nationwide demonstrations. The Hong Kong Flu, unfortunately, was not a news item of high priority.

The medical treatment I had received for the Hong Kong Flu consisted of antibiotics and cough medicine, which had zero effectiveness. That was because antibiotics are ineffective as a treatment against a virus. Only when I had been given steroid drugs and oxygen did I notice an improvement in my condition. Again, the medical profession knew as much about the influenza A virus in 1968 as it knows today about Covid-19. It appears that medical and scientific progress is at a snail's pace when it comes to flus and viruses.

The devastation inflicted on our economy, including the loss of jobs, the interruption of the career paths of recent graduates, and the imposition of travel restrictions have been a gut-punch to Americans. Moreover, our nation's schoolchildren have been irreparably harmed by Covid-19. The health protocols proposed by the CDC for our nation's schools have lacked scientific basis and have not produced any positive results. The fact remains that there is a low probability of a child being infected by Covid-19. In my opinion, there is as much chance of a child being felled by Covid-19 as there is of me winning the state lottery. The low probability of a child being afflicted by Covid-19 is one reason parents have opposed mask mandates for their children. A young child needs to interact with his classmates and teachers. This will enable a child to grow socially, emotionally, and academically. Being

forced to wear a mask the entire day does not promote good

educational and interpersonal skills.

Chapter Three

A New Beginning

1. The Death of Little Black Sambo

Teaching was a far cry from working undercover but it was a welcome challenge. Moreover, I was able to witness first-hand the "management" of our public school system. It was a revelation.

We recited the Pledge of Allegiance each morning at the beginning of the school day. Prayers in school had been ruled unconstitutional in 1962 by the U.S. Supreme Court and therefore were not allowed to be recited in the classroom. Additionally, *The Story of Little Black Sambo* had disappeared from the first-grade curriculum by the end of the 1960s. Change was on the way. However, was it for the better?

Classroom size was determined by the number of desks and chairs one could fit into a classroom. My homeroom accommodated 37 students. There wasn't room for more students. In today's public schools, the number of students in a classroom is generally governed by each city or town's collective bargaining agreement (CBA) negotiated between the teachers' union and the respective school board.

The movement to replace the former pass-fail system of promotion with a system dedicated to the granting of social promotion was underway. However, there were still students in the sixth grade who were 13 and 14, the result of a strict retention policy.

2. How Schools Manipulate Student Records

In the school district in which I had taught, teachers had been ordered by school administrators to scrub student records. All notes that had been made by school personnel and any standardized test scores were to be removed from student files. The appropriateness of such a directive appeared to be in violation of legal statutes. My hesitance to become complicit in the alteration of student records was made manifest to school authorities. The rationale that I had been given by school authorities for this course of action was the fear of potential lawsuits by students and their parents against the town for any unflattering remarks in student files.

In addition, another questionable practice employed by school administrators concerned student attendance. During the school year, teachers were required to meticulously record student absences and tardiness. However, approximately one month before the end of the school year, teachers were ordered to record students as "present" in their school registers for the remainder of the school year. In good conscience, I was unable to carry out the directive. Notwithstanding my objection, those school registers were later certified by school administrators to be true and correct. They were then forwarded to the State Board of Education in Massachusetts.

Why did I refuse to sign-off on my school register? It was because school attendance had been trending downward as we approached the end of the school year. As the weather turned warmer, so did the uptick in truancy. Therefore, I had implored school authorities of the need to be more circumspect in maintaining accurate attendance records in case the local truancy officers asked for verification of student attendance. Furthermore, I added that there may be instances where parents

41

involved in a custodial battle would appreciate accurate attendance records being maintained on their children.

3. Old School vs. New School

My classroom assignment consisted of four sections of social studies (history/geography) classes and one section of science class. The science textbooks which I had been given to distribute to students in my sole science class dated back to World War II. The information was outdated and did not conform to what was being taught in mainstream science classes at that time. Notwithstanding this dilemma, I decided to improvise a science guide for my class. It was both a challenging and rewarding experience. Students were motivated and the results were meritorious.

During the following school year, in partial fulfillment of my obligation to pursue a teaching certificate and maintain my position as an instructor, I had enrolled in an education course at a local college that encouraged innovation in the classroom. One of the techniques being taught involved seating students in groups to maximize achievement. As an example, a group of five students might consist of two "bright" students, two "average" students and one "challenged" student. The idea behind this concept was that the bright students would lead the group and motivate the others which would result in the attainment of greater achievement by all members of the group. It's called the synergistic effect. In sports, we often hear how an exceptionally talented player will make the others around him better. The same principle applies here.

It should be noted that no longer were desks and chairs bolted to a wooden floor in the classroom. Desks and chairs could now be rearranged into whatever order desired by the classroom teacher to seat his or her class. This made it an opportune moment to put into practice the seating of students by groups rather than the traditional method of seating by rows. The students were eager to participate in this new arrangement. However, this was frowned upon by the "old guard" that comprised the rest of the faculty and the principal. The old axiom, "It's difficult to teach an old dog new tricks" can best describe their reaction and receptiveness to new ideas.

4. Taxpayers are Robbed

The remedy proposed by school authorities that would put an end to retention policies that allowed 16-year-olds to be placed in classrooms with 11-year-olds was met with opposition. Some educators believed that it was unethical to grant failing students a "social promotion" to the next grade level. They believed that doing so was testimony to the failure of the public schools to educate those students. Something must be done, they argued, to provide students with the necessary skills to succeed, rather than just issuing them a social promotion. The remedy they proposed was going to be an expensive one for taxpayers.

The plan was to hire additional teachers, so-called specialists. There would be reading specialists, math specialists, and so on. It was obvious that this plan was going to cost taxpayers huge dollars. Whatever issues the classroom teacher was unable to resolve, the student would be referred to a specialist for resolution of his problem. I compare it to having a primary care physician who is unable to cure your malady, referring you to a specialist for diagnosis and treatment.

As more teachers were hired by school boards, school budgets went through the roof. The tax burden on homeowners was enormous. But did the costs justify the results? Several years later, I had spoken to a so-called "reading specialist" and asked her if she had monitored the progress of her former students throughout their high school years. She said she had indeed tracked their "progress". What she then told me sent a chill through my body. She explained that not a single child had achieved a reading level above seventh grade upon graduation from high school. "Bob", she sighed, "the system has been an abject failure." Taxpayer dollars had been flushed down the drain.

5. Love at First Sight

She had blonde hair, blue eyes, and a figure that took your breath away. What wasn't there to like about this young lady? Her name was Elizabeth, a first-year teacher at the school in which I had taught class. The first time we had met, sparks flew as we gazed intimately into each other's eyes. It was as though we were the only two people in the room and time was at a standstill. It's something that you rarely get to experience more than once in your life.

We dated but our time together was tragically cut short. Beth had been complaining of headaches the last weekend we were together and again during the early part of the week. On Wednesday, she came to me at the end of the school day and told me she had collapsed twice in her classroom. She added, in a distressful voice, that the custodian had yelled at her because some of her students had left wads of paper on the floor and scolded her for their actions.

Seeing she was not well, I told her that I would take her to a doctor that I knew who had maintained office hours on Wednesday. It was 1969, and most, if not all physicians' offices were closed on Wednesdays. We were preparing to leave the building when Beth stopped to speak to the school principal. She stated that she would be leaving her car in the school's parking area because she was going with me to seek medical attention. The school principal was unsympathetic to her condition and advised her against leaving her vehicle in the parking area of the school. I interjected that she was in no condition to drive on her own and that I would be taking her to the doctor. In addition, I assured him that the auto would be removed from the school's parking lot later that day. The principal, however, was quite adamant about not leaving the vehicle on school grounds and we engaged in a heated exchange of words. Beth broke down and asked me to stop quarreling with the principal. She didn't want any repercussions from school authorities. Instead, she implored me to follow her back to her apartment.

My efforts to dissuade her from driving home proved fruitless. With great trepidation, I followed her back to her apartment. When we had gotten there, she collapsed on her sofa in exhaustion. She asked me to stay with her and we lay on the sofa, embraced in each other's arms. Suddenly, she appeared listless and unresponsive to my words. Her breathing was slow and shallow accompanied by a weak pulse. My heart began racing, and tears were falling from my eyes. All signs of life then appeared to vanish from her body. Frantically, I administered CPR and tried to revive Beth. She did not respond, however, to my attempts at resuscitation. Bewildered and crying, I held Beth in my arms. The woman I had loved, passed away in my arms that evening. The autopsy report indicated that the cause of death was a brain aneurysm. Beth was 22 years young.

Beth's death made me wonder how someone so young and who had so much to live for could have suddenly departed this world. Beth was a compassionate person, full of energy, and loved by her students. She was 22 and I had just turned 25. We had discussed plans for our future together. Two people but one dream. And in an instant the dream had vanished and lives today only in my memories.

Overwhelmed by her death, I didn't go to school for the next two days and had a substitute teacher cover my classes. When I had returned to school, I was met in my classroom by the custodian and the principal. It was about twenty minutes before the arrival of the students.

The custodian, "Jerkwater Joe", was an ornery and unsociable cuss. He complained about the students not "cleaning up in the room after themselves" during the two days the substitute had covered my classes. Next, the principal, a lazier individual than you would ever meet in your life, who was said to have kept two desks in his office, one for each foot, joined the custodian in reprimanding me for an untidy classroom.

It was at that instance, that I had a defining moment in my life. In a calm manner, I had repeated to them what Beth had told me about the lack of cooperation and harassment by Jerkwater Joe on the day of her death. Next, I reminded the principal of his unwillingness to allow Beth to leave her auto in the school's parking area so I could drive her to a doctor.

My next remarks were spoken in a resounding manner and peppered with rather colorful language. I apprised both the custodian and the principal of my intended actions if I had caught them again in my classroom. They must have believed me because neither one of them set foot in my classroom during my presence for the remainder of the school year.

Naturally, this incident made it all the way up the chain-of-command to the school board. When the board members had heard of the events that had led to my confrontation with the custodian and the principal, they expressed their sympathy. Moreover, I was offered a transfer to another school for the following school year, an increase in salary, and promised tenure at the end of that school year. The board believed that a one-year cooling down period would be mutually beneficial to all parties. The town wanted peace and I had wanted closure. I accepted their offer.

Tenure is no small thing. A teacher, in those days, was awarded tenure after three years of successful teaching experience. It meant that a teacher could not be dismissed without just cause. And just cause was difficult to prove in most cases.

6. To Be or Not to Be: Career Assessment

According to the calendar on my wall it was 1972. Three years had now elapsed since I had begun teaching. Moreover, I had applied for and had received state certification

as a teacher. Furthermore, I had been awarded tenure.
Additionally, during those three years, I had completed my
studies towards a Master's degree from the University of
Massachusetts. The Master's led to another pay raise.

Thankfully, my health had improved to the point where
I had resumed running and working out in the gym. It was time
to reassess my career goals. Did I want to return to Customs or
continue as a teacher?

There had been a restructuring at the Customs
Department and several of my contacts were no longer there or
had moved on to other positions within the agency. Moreover, I
was older than new recruits. Field work was reserved for the
younger hires and I no longer fit the profile. The FBI Director,
J Edgar Hoover, had passed away and significant changes were
about to be made at that agency. Although the Customs
Department was a separate agency from the FBI, the death of
Hoover triggered a ripple effect throughout several federal
agencies. Things would never again be the same in federal law
enforcement.

At a crossroads, I had made my decision. It was to remain a teacher.

7. The Baby Jesus Under Attack

As I had written earlier, prayers in public schools were ruled unconstitutional by the U.S. Supreme Court in 1962. Consequently, teachers could not lead their students in reciting the Lord's Prayer. However, there's an old saying: "give them an inch, and they'll take a foot; give them a foot, and they'll take a yard". Commencing in the early 1970s and continuing to this day, there has been an onslaught against religious freedom brought on by the enemies of Christianity.

Public schools were under attack for calling the school break at the end of the calendar year "Christmas vacation". Instead, the term "winter vacation" was the preferred description. Moreover, teachers initially were discouraged and then outright forbidden from displaying Nativity scenes in their classrooms, including decorations that portrayed Christian symbols. Furthermore, the exchange of Christmas gifts was equally discouraged and then banned by those in opposition to

Christmas. Additionally, Christmas parties were also taboo. Christmas plays and Christmas concerts suffered a similar fate. The iconoclasts based their opposition to Christmas on the unfounded belief that these displays and events violated the doctrine of "separation of church and state".

The school in which I had worked was ordered to forego the singing of Christmas carols at its Christmas concert. It seemed a Jewish organization had gone to court in Massachusetts to block our Christmas pageant. The court order was clear: "no Christmas carols could be sung" during the concert. However, there is an old saying in show business and that is "the show must go on." The dilemma with which we were confronted was how to hold the Christmas concert without violating the court order. Both the teachers and the students worked passionately to ensure a successful concert. To cancel it, would have been a great disappointment.

Several television crews, however, were in town to cover our concert once they had heard we were going to move forward with the event. They were anxious to see how we were going to pull it off without incurring the wrath of a court order.

The chorus, per the court order, did not *sing* any Christmas carols. Instead, the chorus *hummed* the carols. One of the evening newscasters jovially reported that the concert went on as scheduled and turned out to be a real *humdinger*.

8. Mary Jane and Her Cousin Cocaine

Have you ever wondered what takes place at your child's school when they are sent home early because of teachers' workshop day (or some such name)? It was the early 1970s. Students had been dismissed early so that teachers in my school district could participate in a workshop on school discipline. The principal and assistant-principal (called vice-principal or principal of vice at the time) led the discussion. Teachers were asked what their greatest concerns were with regards to discipline. The brainstorming session produced a short list headed by students "chewing gum in class" and their "failure to cover textbooks". When it came my turn to offer a suggestion, I had proposed the need to formulate a district-wide plan to address the growing concerns on drug use among adolescents. My suggestion was summarily dismissed by those in attendance. I was told "get real", "our students don't do that", and "they are too young to understand about drug use". At the end of the session, the administrators informed us to be prepared to offer solutions at our next workshop that would address the issues that had been the focal point of our discussion that day.

It was apparent that school administrators and a good number of faculty were out of touch with recent nationwide developments on drug use among adolescents. Therefore, during the ensuing week, I had decided to put together several classroom activities which would encourage students to participate in an open discussion on drugs. The school nurse supported my efforts.

And then, without warning, as a thief in the night, tragedy struck this idyllic suburban community. A male student who was an attendee at the high school was found dead in his parents' basement. Reports indicated that it had been a suicide, death by hanging. In addition, he had been a victim of drug usage.

After the numbing effect of the initial shock subsided, the town decided to conduct a survey in the schools and obtain feedback on drug use among its students. Predictably, the results raised concerns among the townsfolk. It seemed that a remarkably high number of students had used marijuana, including students at the elementary level. Additionally, hard drugs such as cocaine, had been in use. Consequently, the school board directed the school administrators to address the issue.

At the next monthly teachers' workshop, "gum chewing" and "textbook covers" were verboten topics. Our focal point was to implement a program to address the drug issue. Like good soldiers we brainstormed the session.

Many of my colleagues, especially the elderly teachers, however, were not comfortable discussing drugs with their students. Moreover, the school board expressed misgivings about the ability of those teachers to present a drug program to their class and decided to hire an outside contractor to facilitate the process.

Classroom teachers were evaluated by those consultants to determine our level of competence in presenting a drug program to students. The evaluators had rated me the top teacher in the district. Thanking them, I suggested that they should convey their evaluation of my performance to the school administrators. That they did, wholeheartedly!

Chapter Four

Suffer Little Children

1. Small School Building, Small Problems; Big School Building, Big Problems

During the mid-to-late 1970s, Assumption Public School, was being leased by the town of Bellingham, Massachusetts from the Catholic Church because of overcrowding of the town's public schools. The school, which housed fifth, sixth, and seventh-grade students was a precursor of today's so-called "middle schools". I was assigned to a seventh-grade class at the school. The school was rife with environmental hazards. Those hazards exposed the students and staff at the school to significant dangers which adversely affected their health. Poor drinking water and exposure to asbestos were the culprits. School administrators and board officials, however, were committed to keeping this a secret from the public. The denials, cover-up, and acts of recrimination committed by those in authority are a testament to the lack of accountability for the health and safety of our school children in our nation's schools. It persists to this day.

2. The Big Cover-Up *or* It's Snowing in the Classroom

Snow in the classroom? The ceiling in my classroom had cracked in several places and a powdery substance was falling from the ceiling onto the desks, floor, and students. In fact, when I would arrive at school in the morning, the desks in my classroom were covered with this flaking material, which turned out to be asbestos dust. It was a conspicuous sight. Indeed, you could take your finger and write on the tops of the desks, the same way you would on furniture that was heavily covered with dust. Additionally, students had complained about bits of the flaking substance falling into their hair and eyes.

In January of 1977, I had brought the matter to the attention of the building's Principal, Mr. Joseph DiPietro, aka "lunch-pail Joe" and to its Vice-Principal, Walter Nadolny. My concerns, however, fell on deaf ears.

Before continuing, I should explain the principal's nickname, "lunch-pail Joe". According to the parent of one of my students, the nickname "lunch-pail Joe" was the principal's moniker when he had attended school. Joe was a diminutive youngster and brought a rather oversized lunch box with him to class. Hence, he was given the handle, "lunch-pail Joe" by some of his classmates. Apparently, that nickname had stuck to him like velcro throughout his life.

After having been rebuffed by the building principal, I had voiced my concerns about the hazardous material in my classroom to a member of the school committee who had given me his assurance that the matter would be looked into by the board. One entire year had elapsed, however, and "paralysis of analysis" had set in on the school board. The response from school officials was that they were still looking into the matter.

The teachers' union, which at times, was a rubber-stamp for the policies of school officials, maintained a position of neutrality. There were actually three distinct levels of union membership which comprised the teachers' union; the local branch, simply called, the Bellingham Teachers' Association

(BTA); the state branch, commonly known as, the Massachusetts Teachers' Association (MTA); and the national branch, widely referred to as, the National Education Association (NEA). Not surprisingly, there are many taxpayers who would refer to this triumvirate as an "unholy trinity".

Undeterred by the obstinance of school authorities, I had contacted state health officials in early 1978 about the hazardous material in my classroom. State health officials gave me their assurance that my school building, along with other state buildings, would be included in a test for air quality during that year. Upon completion of those tests, the results had indicated that the building in which I had taught, Assumption Public School, tested at the second highest level for asbestos in the state. So, what did the local school officials do once they had received those results?

The test results were withheld from the public. The school authorities had asked the local media not to publish the results. Moreover, I had learned of this cover-up through a local reporter. The reporter added that if I would consent to an interview on the asbestos problem, she would feel an obligation to respect my First Amendment rights and publish my remarks. She cautioned me that my career could be placed in jeopardy if I had granted her the interview. Notwithstanding her caveat, I replied with strong conviction, that the health and safety of the school children were of paramount importance. My obligation was to the students and their parents, not to school officials.

Once my interview with the reporter had been published and the test results on hazardous asbestos became known, all hell broke loose. In the middle of November 1978, a school committee meeting was held at the Memorial High School auditorium. The auditorium, which seated approximately 400, was filled to capacity. The highly emotional meeting became so heated that at one point the police had to be summoned to thwart possible altercations between parents and town officials.

During the meeting, the supervisor of maintenance for the town's schools had told the parents in the auditorium that he had wanted to conduct his own inspection of the asbestos in the building's ceilings. Therefore, he had proceeded to cut a large hole in the ceiling. He added smugly that he had placed an

63

ordinary bucket under the hole to capture the asbestos dust and

particles. This prompted one parent, who had worked in

building construction to exclaim, *"A bucket can't catch*

asbestos dust! It's very dangerous!" Another parent shouted,

"What kind of fucking idiot would use a bucket to collect

asbestos dust?"

Later that evening, I was accosted by a member of the

school board who proceeded to assault me in front of a group

of taxpayers. A few days later, my automobile had been

vandalized in the school's parking lot. It appeared that someone

had taken a sledgehammer to the front end of the vehicle. From

the appearance of the auto, it looked like I had been in a

collision.

The State Department of Occupation Hazards had

confirmed the unhealthy air at the school, which was due to the

extremely elevated levels of asbestos particles flaking into the

air. In addition, the Special Legislative Commission on

Asbestos indicated that the asbestos level in the air at the

school was more hazardous than had originally been reported

by the health department.

In the face of mounting evidence of a severe health hazard at the school and pressure from parents, school officials decided to close the school for repairs. The building became the first public school building in the U.S. to be shut down for the removal of asbestos. It served as a model for other communities in the U.S.

3. Polluted Drinking Water *or* Water So Toxic That Nemo and Dory Would Not Survive

In addition to the asbestos problem at the school, several children had become ill from drinking the water in the building. I had called attention to the water being unsuitable for drinking at about the same time I had implored school officials to address the asbestos problem. Again, as in the case of unsafe levels of asbestos at the school, school officials turned a blind eye to the problem.

How sick were the children from drinking the water? The students suffered symptoms, such as nausea, vomiting, and intestinal discomfort. Samples of the drinking water were collected by me, and at my own expense, I had the water tested by a private laboratory.

The test results were a cause for concern. Copper levels in the water were found to be six times higher than considered healthful to humans. Additionally, there were other contaminants in the water that were considered unhealthful for consumption.

Subsequently, I submitted the test results to the local school authorities and other town officials. In addition, I referred the matter to the Environmental Protection Agency (EPA). The remedy offered by town officials was to turn on the bubblers or drinking fountains and let them run all day. Of course, this had little or no effect on the quality of the water and did not solve the problem.

It was not until 1991, approximately thirteen years after I had called attention to unsafe drinking water in our public schools, that the EPA published a regulation to reduce the levels of copper and lead in drinking water. Indeed, government moves slowly through its bureaucracy. The regulation is known as the Lead and Copper Rule.

Notwithstanding the EPA regulation, however, unsafe drinking water continues to plague thousands of communities across our nation. And children continue to be the primary victims of this malady.

4. Sins of the Church - Bad Clergy Men

The Rectory, which housed the clergy of Assumption Parish, was adjacent to the school. Some of the male students at Assumption School had served as altar boys at the parish. Unfortunately for those altar boys, one member of the clergy, who could not control his inner demons, violated their innocence.

Shame on the clergy for their misdeeds! And shame on church officials for their role in the cover-up of those abuses!

5. The Sinners

The late Rev. Paul M. Desilets was accused by a group of former altar boys and other male plaintiffs of molesting them for approximately a decade while he was a member of the clergy at the Assumption Parish in Bellingham, Massachusetts between 1974 and 1984. In 2005, Desilets pleaded guilty to molesting 18 boys and was sentenced to 1 1/2 years in prison, followed by 10 years' probation. In addition, he was also ordered to register as a sex offender. He was released from prison in 2006 and returned to his order in Quebec, Canada. Desilets passed away in 2010.

A new priest, the Rev. Robert Morrissette, was assigned to Assumption Parish in Bellingham, Massachusetts in 1984 following the departure of Desilets. Morrissette was transferred to Bellingham from another parish by the Archdiocese of Boston after he had admitted to molesting a boy. Additionally, complaints from two other youngsters were issued against Morrissette. You would think he would have learned a lesson from his past immoral behavior. However, during his tenure in Bellingham, the "good reverend" kept pornographic material, visited homosexual areas in Key West, Florida, and had an affair with another man.

A higher authority.
St. Peter's Basilica. Illustration by Jean-Pol Grandmont on September 29, 2011.
Wikimedia Commons.

6. The Enablers

When you read about the activities of the Rev. Paul M.

Desilets and the Rev. Robert Morrissette, it makes you wonder

how they were able to continue their lifestyle for such a long

length of time without raising suspicions from members of the

Assumption Parish, or in the case of the Rev. Desilets, from

school authorities. So, let's examine comments about those

priests from a church parishioner who also happened to be a

school administrator.

According to an article by Parker Waichman LLP titled,

"More Priest Abuse in Bellingham", [4] church documents that

---

[4] Parker Waichman LLP. (n.d.). *More Priest Abuse in Bellingham.*
Retrieved October 18,2021, from
https://www.yourlawyer.com/sexual-abuse-3/more-priest-abuse-in-bellingham/

had been released indicated that a priest (Morrissette) who had

been assigned to Assumption Parish in Bellingham in 1984 had

been sent there,

> "... to escape his record of sexual abuse at another
>
> parish...."[5] "The documents also show that Boston's
>
> Cardinal Bernard Law was aware of far more clergy
>
> abuse cases than he has admitted, and his
>
> predecessor, Cardinal Humberto Medeiros, covered
>
> up for molesters, too".[6]

The article then cited one of the school administrators

in Bellingham, Mr. Joseph DiPietro (aka "lunch-pail Joe"),

who had also served as a "lector" at the parish for a number of

years, on the behavior of Morrissette. DiPietro opined,

> "I never had the slightest hint of him doing anything
>
> wrong. I never noticed that he was in any way
>
> improper."[7]

Really? And what about Desilets, who had

preceded Morrissette? According to this same school

administrator and lector at the parish,

---

[5] Ibid.
[6] Ibid.
[7] Ibid.

In other words, "hear no evil, speak no evil, see no evil". Or could this have been the makings of another cover-up?

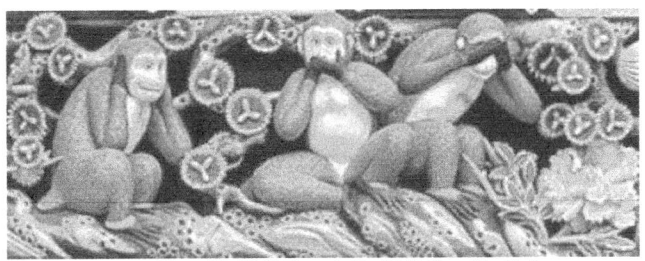

Hear No Evil, Speak No Evil, See No Evil.
Carving on the statue of Tosho-gu Shrine, Nikko, Japan. By Ray in Manila -
https://www.flickr.com/photos/rayinmanila/42687150801/, CC BY 2.0, https://commons.wikimedia.org/w/index.php?curid=82531971

7. A Good Idea Gone Bad - Shut Down This Building

From the onset, Assumption School had been beset with problems. The high level of asbestos and the contaminated drinking water had posed substantial dangers to the health of the students who had attended the school. In addition, the parish clergy's betrayal to the altar boys who had attended the school posed an additional risk to their safety.

---

[8] Ibid.

Notwithstanding the repairs to remove the asbestos from the building, in the best interests of the town, it was finally decided to close the school. Its memories, or should we say, *nightmares*, will not be easily forgotten by those who had been in attendance.

8. Retaliation and Racism: Enter "The Hatchet Man" and "Attila the Nun"

Certain school and town officials had been exposed for their participation in the cover-up and overall lack of cooperation with regards to the asbestos and drinking water problems at the Assumption School. Moreover, I had been assaulted by a member of the school board and my vehicle had been vandalized by unknown assailants. Furthermore, after I had alerted school authorities to "keep an eye" on the priest at the Assumption Parish, I was informed that I was no longer welcomed to teach at the Assumption School. Consequently, school officials had me transferred to another school in town, the Macy School, and had assigned me to teach a seventh-grade class.

A new Superintendent of Schools, Peter Vangel, aka *"The Hatchet Man"*, had recently been appointed by the school board to become its chief school administrator. He came with baggage. The disgruntled school administrator had been voted down by the school board in a neighboring city for its position of superintendent of schools. As a fallback, he had applied for the position of superintendent of schools in Bellingham. His marching orders were clear: to scrutinize my performance so that the school board would have grounds on which to terminate my employment.

In order to assist the superintendent in his efforts, the school board had hired a new principal at the Macy School. The principal was a former nun who had either resigned from the order or had been expelled from it in an unceremonious manner. Rumors had persisted that the latter may have been the case. Whatever the reason for her leaving the order, however, it had left its mark on her and earned her the title, *"Attila the Nun"*. She was strictly bad news.

Initially, the game plan was to place a listening device in my classroom and have the secretary to the principal record my comments. When this failed to produce anything detrimental to my teaching performance, a new strategy was employed in the following school year. The plan was to have me teach all the subjects in my seventh-grade class. This meant that the students in my classroom would not change classes for different subjects, as was customarily the case. Moreover, in certain subject areas, such as science, no textbooks were provided to the students. When I had requested textbooks for the class, I was told, "You're a smart guy, you don't need textbooks to teach a class." Well, that may have been true, but students needed a textbook and a workbook to complete their assignments in science.

In addition, I had been assigned to a classroom in one corner of the school building. The intent was to isolate the students in my classroom from having contact with students from other classrooms at the school. Consequently, students ate lunch alone and went to recess in a restricted area of the playground with no access to the playground equipment. We had been ostracized by *"Attila the Nun"*.

Moreover, all the African-American students in the seventh-grade at the Macy School had been assigned to my classroom in order to segregate them from their peers. Another faculty member had informed me that the other seventh-grade teachers did not want the African-American students assigned to their classes, as they were deemed to be troublemakers. Racism had indeed reared its ugly head at the school.

The bottom line was that school authorities along with influential members of the governing class in Bellingham had deemed me to be a threat to their power structure and wanted me to leave town. They were unable to terminate my employment for lack of cause and instead embarked upon a scorched earth policy of harassing tactics. Additionally, they committed the unconscionable act of making the lives of children assigned to my classroom less than a pleasurable experience. Shameful!

9. Big Brother

A new era was about to begin in education. It was the early 1980s and public schools were in a nationwide crisis.

They were suffering from both a lack of leadership and the

arrival of a new generation of teachers who were found to be

lacking in basic skills.

Former President James Carter signed into law the

Department of Education Organization Act in October of 1979,

which had the effect of creating the Department of Education

(DoEd). The DoEd officially began operating in May of 1980.

Carter's intentions were more political theater than

having anything to do with improving education. In 1980,

Carter was seeking a second term as president. In addition, he

was reaching out to the teachers' unions for their support.

Notwithstanding the support of the teachers' unions, Carter lost

the election rather handily to Ronald Reagan.

During the presidential campaign of 1980, Reagan

insisted that government was the problem and not the solution

to issues facing our nation, including our schools. Reagan had

vowed to dismantle the Department of Education if he were

elected president. Once in office, however, he found that

attempting to abolish the Department of Education proved to

be an insurmountable task. Reagan even found opposition from people within his own administration. Finally, he decided that the game was something he couldn't win.

The newly minted Department of Education, concomitantly, with the large and vocal teachers' unions were now in charge of our public schools. What that meant for school districts across the U.S. was that once you had accepted federal dollars for education you must also accept federal law and regulations that govern education. School policy would no longer be determined at the state and local levels; it would be mandated by the federal government in collaboration with the teachers' unions.

Sadly, students continued to be "promoted" from one grade level to the next grade level, notwithstanding their lack of basic skills. Reading and math scores continued to plummet precipitously. A high school diploma had lost its significance. Once upon a time, employers would ask an applicant, "Do you have a high school diploma?" Having a high school diploma indicated that a person had a skill set and would most likely be able to satisfactorily perform his or her job functions. Now, those employers recognizing the loss in value of a high school diploma, had to administer tests to an applicant to determine if he or she could read, write, and perform basic math operations. No longer could an employer rely solely upon a high school diploma to attest as to whether a person had viable skills.

Another culprit in the new era of education were the publishing houses. Those companies had updated their catalogs that were being marketed to educators for use in the classroom. As I was perusing one of the catalogs I had received, I was startled to find books titled, *My Daddy Has a Boyfriend* and *Mommy Has a Girlfriend.* And even more shocking, those books were recommended for first and second graders.

In 1983, the U.S. National Commission on Excellence in Education issued a report titled, "A Nation at Risk: The Imperative for Educational Reform". The report was a strong condemnation of our nation's failing public schools. The Democrats advocated for increased federal aid to address the problems in our schools. President Reagan, on the other hand, stated that the problems with our schools could be solved by demanding excellence from our students and improving the quality of teaching. Moreover, he was an advocate of merit pay to reward outstanding teachers.

10. University Bound

After years of diligent and conscientious teaching, it was time to re-examine my career goals. It was evident that the town of Bellingham had a leadership crisis within its education system. School administrators defended the system's status quo in the face of mounting evidence that there was a need for reform. Change was urgently needed in order to offer students a better education for a better future. The school administrators talked about excellence but only offered students despair and disappointment.

Rather than continue to lock horns with a group of challenged school administrators who had failed to prioritize the educational needs and safety of its students, I had accepted a position at the university level. Additionally, I conducted numerous seminars and offered workshops to the general public.

Although I was no longer employed in the public school system, I continued to monitor the crisis in education. New ideas were being offered as a prescription to cure the ills that plagued our nation's schools. And, of course, taxpayer dollars were being expended on our educational system, the way a drunken sailor spends money at a bar. Not that it did any good, as we shall discover in the following chapters.

Chapter Five

Attempts to Fix Our Schools

1. "Just Say No to Drugs"

In 1982, First Lady Nancy Reagan had visited an elementary school while on a speaking tour. A young girl had raised her hand and asked the former first lady what she should do if someone offered her drugs. Mrs. Reagan responded that she should "just say no". And so, the "Just Say No to Drugs" movement was born.

Nancy Reagan speaking to a group of students at a "Just Say No" rally at the White House. May 22, 1986. From the National Archives Catalog. White House Photographic Collection. Reagan White House Photographs.

Subsequently, in 1986, President Reagan issued a proclamation that kicked off the very first official "Just Say No to Drugs Week". In that same year, Mrs. Reagan, during a televised address to the nation, had spoken about her times travelling throughout the country promoting her anti-drug campaign. She implored her listeners to remain steadfast in their opposition to drugs. Furthermore, she added these memorable words that best defined the movement, "Say yes to your life. And when it comes to drugs and alcohol just say no."[9]

The president and first lady's messages were clear but was it too late? Would America "Just Say No to Drugs"? In response, educational programs were diligently employed in our schools. Furthermore, media campaigns were launched nationwide to stem the use of drugs among adults. In the short-term, the effort produced encouraging results. In the long-term, however, it was a far different story.

---

[9] Landmark Recovery. (2018, December 3). *Just Say No And Its Effects.* Retrieved December 27, 2021, from https://landmarkrecovery.com/just-say-no-and-its-effects/

In addition, the ensuing "drug wars" took its toll. The cost to control the smuggling of drugs into the U.S. was immense both in tax dollars and in human lives.

2. Saying No to Drugs is Easier Said Than Done

During my lifetime, I never engaged in recreational drugs. Long before former First Lady Nancy Reagan's message of, "Just Say No to Drugs", I was already saying, "NO!". My regimen was a fairly simple one. It was to exercise regularly, refrain from smoking cigarettes, and follow a healthy diet. After I had graduated from college, drinking beer and smoking cigars had lost its allure. At dinner, I now enjoyed an occasional glass of wine. Moreover, when I was in a social gathering, scotch and water (or scotch on the rocks) was my preferred libation. This was all done in moderation.

For many people, however, it was difficult to resist the temptation of recreational drugs amid pressure from their peers. Several persons I had known fell victim to drugs and in some cases the price they had paid altered their lives. Here are some of those unfortunate stories.

Case #1. My senior prom date. Several of my friends had sisters who had wanted to date me when I was in high school. One of these girls, whom I will call Mary, was tall, attractive, and in her junior year. Without hesitation, she accepted my invitation to the senior prom. After high school, however, we went our separate ways. Mary had gone to nursing school and became a registered nurse. Then, something went wrong. According to the account of events that I had received, Mary had attended a party and had "dropped acid" (slang for LSD). Lysergic acid diethylamide (LSD) is a potent hallucinogen that can cause some serious side effects. In Mary's case, it "blew her mind" (slang for caused severe mental impairment).

Mary could no longer continue her nursing career. Instead, she went back home to live with her father who had been entrusted with her care. Moreover, Mary was also under psychiatric care. As time went on, Mary had shown improvement. Her nursing career was over, but she was allowed to drive a motor vehicle, which was probably a huge mistake. One day while stopped at an intersection, Mary flipped out of her mind. She had left her auto and ran screaming into the intersection. Not surprisingly, Mary was returned to the psychiatric ward at a local hospital for evaluation and treatment. While in the hospital, however, she somehow managed to make her way to the male patients area of the ward. She had brought some men's magazines with her with which to entice the male patients. Poor sweet Mary, my date to the senior prom.

Mary's life, however, did take a turn for the better. There's an old saying, "there is someone for everyone". As Mary entered middle age, somebody did come along and asked for her hand in marriage. Miraculously, Mary did live into her early seventies. She had a peaceful death.

All Mary had to do was say "NO!" to drugs. Whatever the reason, "no" was not part of her vocabulary on that fateful evening when she had "tripped out on acid".

Case #2. A schoolteacher with secrets. Let's call her Abby. She was a public school teacher whom I had met at a party. During the time we had dated, I never knew her to smoke tobacco or any other substance. She did, however, enjoy an occasional drink. Surprisingly, she was a pretty kinky lady. Abby had all sorts of sex toys that she had kept in her apartment. At times her apartment resembled an adult entertainment store. That should have sent out a signal to me that there was something going on with her that didn't fit the schoolteacher profile. Who exactly was this woman?

One Saturday evening, after I had returned home from a week-long business trip, we had planned to go out for dinner. Upon arriving at her apartment, I found her in bed struggling to speak in a cohesive manner. It was 6:00 pm. According to Abby, she had been in bed the entire day. She then confessed to what had taken place the previous evening. Abby had visited her "girlfriend" and the two of them had partied that evening. Moreover, the girls had been doing lines of cocaine and had taken Abby's sex toys out for a test drive. Wow! After one-year of dating somebody, you think you know the person, but then you discover that you really don't know them that well.

Abby went on to tell me that her nose was completely numb. She moaned, "It feels a lot like when a dentist gives you a shot of Novocaine to freeze your jaw before he begins to drill your tooth."

With great urgency, I had offered to take Abby to the hospital, but she declined to go there and seek assistance. My next suggestion was to help her out of bed and walk her around the apartment in an effort to improve her circulation. That also fell on deaf ears. Fortunately, the worse was already over and Abby made a full recovery.

Abby is another instance of somebody failing to just say "NO!" to drugs. She had a scare that day but survived the ordeal.

Case #3. A good friend from high school named Winston. My 50th high school class reunion gave me the opportunity to reconnect with friends whom I had not seen in decades. There were few, if any, of my former classmates that I would have recognized at the reunion, were it not for the name and photo tags that we were given to wear at the event. As I had entered the reception area, an attractive lady had approached me and without uttering a single syllable embraced me with a passionate kiss. After exchanging pleasantries, I had thought back to the last time I had seen her prior to the reunion. It was after our high school graduation ceremony when we had returned our caps and gowns. Aside from the custodial and office staff, we were the only persons in the building. It was then, as a final farewell, we had embraced each other in a long passionate kiss. A warm embrace and passionate kiss between two high school graduates renewed fifty years later at a class reunion. An element of déjà vu or just mere happenstance?

Now to Winston and his sad story. Winston and I had seen each other occasionally in the early years after high school; however, we had not been in contact with each other for the past forty years. During that time, Winston went to college, got married, had children, and worked as an engineer. Unfortunately, he could not bring himself to just say "NO!" when a sinister lady entered his life and had taken control of it to his detriment. She went by many names. Some called her Mary Jane, Aunt Mary, weed, grass, and pot. However, her common scientific name is cannabis or marijuana.

Winston went on in detail of how he had been introduced to marijuana and how addicted he had become to the drug. His addiction reached the point where he would spend the entire day smoking pot. Winston's wife had divorced him and he had lost his job. He explained how he had sought help for his addiction and was finally able to, in his own words, "get the monkey off my back". It was a long road to recovery, but Winston emerged victorious over his nemesis. Moreover, he had remarried and had found another job. It was a very compelling story and a heartwarming ending to what could have been a very unfortunate outcome. Sadly, the same cannot be said for so many others who were unable to just say "NO!" to drugs.

There you have it reader. Three incidents of drug use that underscore the pain and hardship brought about by the use of drugs. Those drugs included LSD, cocaine, and marijuana. The users of the drugs were not bad people. A registered nurse, a teacher, and an engineer were their chosen professions. All were intelligent people. Notwithstanding their positions in life, each of them were unable to resist the toxic allure of recreational drugs.

3. Legalization of Marijuana

Marijuana laws have been enacted at a rapid pace in the U.S., thereby making it difficult to keep up with all the new legislation. From medical use to recreational use, different states have their own laws regulating the use of marijuana. As of February 2021, there are only eight states where marijuana is fully illegal. Those states are Alabama, Idaho, Kansas, Nebraska, North Carolina, South Carolina, Tennessee, and Wyoming. Some states permit the use of marijuana only for medical reasons. On the other hand, other states allow the use of marijuana for recreational purposes. In some jurisdictions, marijuana is permitted for both medical and recreational usage.

Although the closing chapter on drugs in the U.S. has not been written, it appears that the campaign to "Just Say No to Drugs" has lost its staying power. Furthermore, opioid use is now the main threat facing our nation. School programs that once warned of the hazards of the use of drugs are no longer in vogue. Rather, priority is given to programs dealing with

"Black Lives Matter", "Holocaust Studies", and the "LGBT Agenda".

4. Recertification of Teachers

When I had received my license to teach school in the state of Massachusetts, it was a "life-time" license. It did not require an annual or periodic renewal. In general, this was the licensing requirement for teachers throughout the U.S. In 1983, however, the U.S. National Commission on Excellence in Education issued a report titled, "A Nation at Risk: The Imperative for Educational Reform". Based on the recommendations in that report, there was a clamor for improving the quality of teaching in the U.S.

Ten years later, in 1993, words took the form of action. In Massachusetts, the Massachusetts Education Reform Act of 1993, required that all educators had to undergo recertification in order to remain active for employment. In addition, those teaching certificates needed to be renewed every five years.

It is now customary practice throughout our nation, that teachers renew their certification every five years. No longer can teachers enjoy the luxury of having a lifetime certificate.

Licensing boards throughout the U.S. require members of other professions to maintain a license to practice their trade and offer their services to the public. So why not educators?

Notwithstanding the licensing requirements imposed on educators, the teaching profession continues to be plagued by less than competent teachers. There is a constant clamor for a return to basics in education. In years past, the basic skills were referred to as the "3 Rs" or "Reading, Writing, and Arithmetic".

During my early years in teaching, the town in which I had been employed had begun to test its students in reading and math skills. School leaders had proclaimed the testing period as "Competency Testing Week". In order to generate an awareness and an understanding of the program, parents were invited to meet their child's teachers at their respective schools to discuss the tests. The school in which I had worked was hosting the discussion of the program during the evening. As I had approached the entrance to the school, there was a huge

banner draped across the front of the building with the words,

"Competentcy Testing Week". The spelling of one of the

words in the banner immediately caught my eye. Entering the

building, I had confronted the members of the staff responsible

for the banner and pointed out the incorrect spelling of

"competency". Panic gripped the staff. "Take it down!",

someone exclaimed excitedly. There were no custodians on

hand that evening and I sure as heck was not going to climb a

ladder to remove the banner from the building in the darkness.

Good luck to that idea! Therefore, the banner remained in place

for public view. Parents, school board members, and the local

media were not impressed with teachers making spelling

errors. The next day's edition of the local newspaper was also

not very forgiving of the poorly spelled word on the banner.

The media watchdogs mockingly suggested that the town may

be better served by initially testing their own educators before

testing its school children. Teachers' faces turned red with

embarrassment. To make matters worse, the teachers' union

was in contract negotiations with the school board on a new contract. How do you justify asking for a raise after that fiasco?

If teachers of yesteryear displayed moments of incompetence, educators of today fare no better in their lack of basic skills. Indeed, the incompetence level of modern educators may be unparalleled in the history of our nation's educational system.

The "3 Rs" are no less important today than they were generations ago. When educators cannot display a mastery of the three basic skills (reading, writing, and arithmetic), then how can we expect them to instruct our children to achieve success in those areas? Despite the recertification of teachers every five years, the results have not supported the effort.

What have been the impediments to hiring competent instructors? One, online classes are no replacement for in-person attendance in a walled classroom. Teaching programs that allow for remote learning do not prepare educators for a career in the classroom. Two, texting and emails have diminished a person's ability to write in an effective manner. As a result, teachers are being hired who have low communication skills. Three, the hiring of minorities who have attended inferior colleges. Affirmative action hires do not bring the best and brightest teachers to the classroom. Fourth, the failure to attract "smart" people into the teaching profession. Why would somebody choose a career in teaching when there are better career opportunities? Fifth, the inability to retain good teachers.

What can be done to improve teacher competence? One, universities should offer education programs that require in-person learning. Remote learning does not allow for the proper interaction between students and their professors or among their classmates.

Two, teaching programs should emphasize that graduates demonstrate proficiency in writing. Too many students who graduate from college today are unable to properly construct a sentence or a paragraph. Moreover, their grammar and spelling reveal glaring deficiencies in their command of the English language. A common excuse among teachers from disciplines other than English is "I'm not an English teacher. It's no big thing if I can't spell or write effectively." Wrong! Notwithstanding their major discipline, teachers are responsible for demonstrating proficient writing skills to their students. Otherwise, expect bad habits to beget bad habits. For example, a student who has had a Business Math instructor who cannot write effectively will most probably develop poor communication skills as a result of that instructor's influence. What good does it do a graduate if he or she can perform business math operations but cannot draft a report to effectively communicate the results of a business forecast to the company's chief financial officer? Writing does matter!

Three, school districts should recruit graduates from universities that have well established education programs. School boards need to resist the pressure to recruit affirmative action hires. For example, in the Florida county in which I reside, the federal government paid a visit to our school board because of complaints it had received about the lack of teachers of color. The federal authorities threatened to withhold federal funds unless the school board agreed to hire more teachers of color. Not surprisingly, the school board complied with the request of the government. Forcing a school board to hire affirmative action applicants under the threat of withholding federal funds is an infringement on a school department's right to recruit and retain the best and brightest teachers. It is an example of government overreach that threatens to destroy our nation's schools.

Four, one way to attract "smart" people into teaching is for school districts to offer "merit pay" in addition to its traditional salary structure. Teachers should be rewarded with a salary commensurate with their outstanding performance. Educators need to know that those who go that extra mile will be compensated for their efforts. Merit pay is one factor in which college graduates would likely weigh the prospect of a career in education favorably.

There is nothing new, however, about offering merit pay to reward and retain good teachers. In fact, former President Ronald Reagan advocated that merit pay should be considered as a reward to teachers for outstanding performance.

Additionally, potential hires should be made aware of opportunities for vertical promotion (such as a principalship) in a school district. Furthermore, it should be emphasized that those opportunities would be based on their qualifications and not on nepotism.

Five, the retention of good teachers. In addition to the aforementioned incentives such as merit pay and opportunities for promotion, few teachers will want to remain in education unless there is an improvement in student discipline.

During my years as a student, the principal was always the most feared authority figure in the school. The least desirable place in which a student could find himself was the principal's office. The buck stopped at the door of the principal's office. A student knew that nothing good would come from a trip to the office of the principal. Teachers taught their lessons. Principals maintained law and order. Discipline was maintained in this type of school culture.

Fast forward to the present day. Students have no fear of teachers. That should come as no surprise! Neither do students, however, have any fear of school administrators. Now

98

that should come as a surprise! Principals, assistant-principals, or whatever title that precedes their name, have lost command of their schools. In sports, when a coach no longer has the respect of his players, we say he or she has "lost control of the locker room". That is enough to get a coach relieved of his duties. If schools were locker rooms, then a principal's employment would suffer a similar fate as that of a coach. However, schools are not locker rooms, and no matter how poor the discipline is in schools, principals are rarely fired from their jobs.

The usual course of action is to lay the blame at the foot of the instructors. Excuses such as, "the teacher's class is not interesting so students are bored" or "the teacher must be firmer in dealing with suspected troublemakers" are usually commonplace among school administrators. It's called "passing the buck".

It is easier for school administrators to blame staff rather than enforce discipline in the schools. It also avoids lawsuits from parents and radical groups. And that makes for a contented school board.

In life, there are events that we experience which defy human comprehension. We don't expect them to occur, however, in a classroom. The following is one such event.

After I had decided to semi-retire, an opportunity presented itself as a substitute teacher in the public schools. At first, I had been a bit hesitant of the offer. Upon reflection, however, I had viewed this as an opportunity to compare education of today with that of my days as a full-time teacher twenty-five years earlier.

One day, I had been assigned to teach a math class at a high school in my county. During the class period, there were two students who continuously walked around the classroom. They were not very responsive to any of my questions. Aside from their walking about the room, however, they did not cause any kind of disturbance. At the end of class, I had approached one of the administrators in the building and apprised him of the situation. He told me he was aware of those students and not to be concerned with the incident.

The next time I had substituted at the school, I spoke to the math teacher whose class I had covered where the students performed a "walk-about" during the class period. He explained that the two students in question "do that every day" and that they were "convicted felons" but due to their ages were given suspended sentences in lieu of prison. I then inquired as to what action the principal had taken regarding those students. The teacher replied, "nothing". He added that he was told to ignore them (the student-felons) unless they became a disturbing influence.

Incomprehensible is the word that best describes the handling of those student-felons. It is a clear case of school authorities not only failing to maintain discipline but also failing to create an atmosphere conducive to learning in the classroom.

Yes, merit pay is important to the retention of good teachers. In addition, opportunities for advancement are important. Besides money and opportunities for promotion, however, teacher morale is a crucial factor in the retention of good educators. Discipline in our schools can help improve morale among the teaching staff. That is the responsibility of school administrators who must set the tone for providing good discipline in our schools. Local school boards must make it clear that they will not accept poor discipline in schools.

5. No Child Left Behind

Another recommendation made by the U.S. National Commission on Excellence in Education was the need to encourage excellence from students. Unfortunately, change in education is an extremely slow process. Therefore, it was not until 2002 that student performance was finally given its long overdue attention by educators.

The No Child Left Behind Act (NCLB) was approved by Congress with strong bipartisan support in 2001 and was signed into law by President George W. Bush in January of 2002. The law required individual states to administer standardized tests to students in our public schools, primarily in reading and math. The principal aim of this act was to measure student performance. It also included holding teachers and school districts accountable for the results.

There is an old adage: "Some people can bring out the best in you, whereas other people bring out the worse in you".

That principle can be applied to describe the influence that a teacher has on his or her students. To wit, poorly trained teachers can have a detrimental effect on the level of achievement of their students. On the other hand, highly motivated and knowledgeable instructors can guide students in their pursuit towards educational excellence.

Better teachers make better students. However, that is not to say students should be given a free pass from being held accountable for their performance. Nor should their parents. Good study skills must be encouraged at home. Parents need to be apprised of the importance of fostering a home environment conducive to good learning. Moreover, objectives must be clearly established based on input from teachers, students, and parents. Student performance can then be measured by objective testing and observation.

6. Assault on Standardized Testing

As long as standardized tests can be administered in an objective and fair manner, they may be useful tools to measure student performance and ability. Testing can identify both strengths and weaknesses of students. Students with strong skill sets may be assigned to more advanced classes where they can be challenged to maximize their potential. On the other hand, specialized programs of instruction may be designed to facilitate growth among students with weak skill sets.

Standardized testing, however, has come under assault from teachers' unions, school administrators, and the so-called "cancel culture" activists. It is clear why teachers' unions and school administrators dislike testing of students' performance. That is because when students fail to attain certain benchmarks, it reflects poorly on teachers, school administrators, and school districts.

On the other hand, the "cancel culture" activists dislike standardized testing because they view it as a discriminatory practice. To those persons, standardized tests are part of a system of "systemic racism", "white supremacy", "neo-colonialism", "white privilege", "cultural bias" and "class warfare".

A colleague of mine was teaching a class titled, Introduction to Statistics, in the evening school at a local university. He was explaining the various ways to calculate an "average" such as the mean, median, and mode. One of his students, a black male, became exasperated because of his inability to grasp the concepts. The student exclaimed, "This is a White man's invention!" Really? That student probably best exemplified the mindset of those who believe that mathematics is somehow part of "systemic racism".

Notwithstanding the objections from teachers' unions, school authorities, and "cancel culture" activists, standardized testing does level the playing field for all students. It allows them to demonstrate their talents regardless of socio-economic status, race, gender, and religion. The SAT tests that are administered at the high school level to college bound students, for example, provide an indication of a student's potential for success by measuring their skills in math, reading, and grammar. In addition to a student's grade point average (GPA), SAT scores are another criteria that universities consider in determining if a student's application for admission should be granted approval.

Less affluent students, for example, have an opportunity to impress college admission boards of their potential for success by their performance on SAT tests. It may be their one chance to gain admission into college. On the other hand, students from wealthy families have always been able to gain admission into college by courtesy of their families' endowments and even outright payments to members of college admission boards. Furthermore, SAT scores are a far more equitable measure for admission to college than is admission by affirmative action. Affirmative action, on the other hand, is employed to satisfy quotas based on government decrees and serves to deprive a worthy student of an opportunity to attend college.

Chapter Six

Where has Civics Instruction Gone?

Do you remember taking a class in civics instruction? Civics was once a key component of the curriculum in the public schools. It was considered a cornerstone in the preparation of students to become good citizens.

We were taught about our three branches of government, namely, the executive branch, the legislative branch, and the judicial branch. We learned how the president, as representative of our executive branch, wore many "hats", each of which signified his responsibility as the leader of our nation. For example, there was the "hat" he wore as commander-in-chief. Congress was our legislative branch, and its duty was to make laws that governed us. The Supreme Court was our judicial branch. Its responsibility was to interpret our laws to make sure they did not violate our Constitution and our individual rights.

In addition, we were told that it was important that we

should all participate in our political process. This included

writing letters to our leaders on important issues, voting, and

getting involved in community activities.

Up until the 1960s, civics was presented either as a

separate course or as part of U.S. history in junior high school

(referred to as middle school today) and in senior high school.

However, beginning in the 1970s, civics began to lose its

standing as an important subject area in our public schools.

What had contributed to this demotion? We will address that

question in the in the remainder of this chapter.

1. Diary of Anne Frank

The Diary of Anne Frank may be considered a

forerunner to the Holocaust studies programs which are now

mandated in many of our public schools. For those readers who

are not familiar with the personage of Anne Frank, she was a

Holocaust victim of World War II. Anne Frank kept a personal

diary during the time in which she and her family had hid from

German soldiers. Eventually, the Franks were arrested and sent

to German concentration camps.

The Diary of Anne Frank was mandatory reading in my eighth grade English class. It was a very compelling story. There was, however, something about the written novel that was troublesome to many of my classmates. It did not appear to have been written by a person who was alleged to have been fourteen to fifteen years old at the time of its writing. We were correct! History has proven that to be the case.

The edition of the novel which I had been required to read credited Anne Frank as the sole author. However, in the version that is read today, called the definitive edition, Otto H. Frank is listed as a co-author. The definitive version of Anne's diary claims to contain approximately thirty percent additional material that had been left out of the original version.

Who is Otto Frank? Otto Frank was the patriarch of the Frank family (Anne's father). With the exception of Otto, all other members of the Frank family had perished in the concentration camps. Anne died at the age of fifteen from typhus at Bergen Belsen concentration camp in 1945. After the war, Otto learned that several pages of Anne's diary had been secured by two of his employees who had planned to return them to Anne after the war. Since Anne had perished at Bergen Belsen, they handed the pages of the diary to Otto. In an interview, Otto claimed that he had known that Anne had kept a diary. He went on to state that he was incredibly surprised about some of the things she had written and that it was quite a different daughter than the one he had known all those years. At the conclusion of the interview, Otto lamented that he believed that most parents do not really know their children.

The original version of *The Diary of Anne Frank* led its readers to believe that it was written entirely by Anne. We know today that Otto edited and rewrote it, either alone or in collaboration with others. Otto included material about Anne's infatuation with Peter van Pels, who was an annex dweller where Anne had been hiding with her parents. On the other hand, Otto censored her diary by excluding passages in which his daughter was critical of her parents' marriage, her sexuality, and her often unflattering comments about her friends, family members, acquaintances, and classmates. He also removed references she had made regarding same sex attraction and scatology (the study of feces). Gross!! One of the last entries written by Anne in her diary states that she didn't get the reputation of being a "little bundle of contradictions" without good reason.

It is those passages which have called into question the character of Anne Frank. Who was the real Anne Frank? Moreover, the editing performed by her father and others who may have assisted him, have cast doubt on whether the diary was the genuine work of Anne. Furthermore, I have seen accounts which have stated that the pages of the diary had been written in ballpoint pen. What is wrong with using ballpoint ink? The problem is ballpoint pens did not come into widespread usage until *after* WWII. The diary was written *during* WWII.

My purpose is not to contest the authenticity of *The Diary of Anne Frank*. It has been a widely controversial diary. There have been lawsuits over it and claims that the diary is a fraud. It is what it is, however, and I will not pass judgment on its veracity. For purposes of my writing, *The Diary of Anne Frank*, introduced generations of students to the horror known as the Holocaust. Additionally, it was one of the precursors of today's Holocaust studies.

2. Jewish Holocaust

In 1978, a four-part miniseries titled, *Holocaust*, was presented on nationwide television. It portrayed the saga of a fictitious Jewish family, the Weiss, and their struggle to survive in Nazi Germany. The series won several awards. Additionally, it drew both praise and criticism. Ironically, criticism came from Holocaust survivor Elie Wiesel, who claimed it was an insult to both those who had perished and to those who had survived during their time in the concentration camps.

Notwithstanding the criticisms, the series had a tremendous impact in public debates on the Holocaust in West Germany and in the U.S. In the U.S., it provided further impetus to the movement mandating Holocaust instruction in our public schools.

Beginning in 1994, the Florida legislature passed the Holocaust Education Bill which required all school districts to incorporate lessons on the Holocaust as part of public-school instruction. That mandate now extends to grades K-12. The website for the Florida Department of Education states the following:

> *"In Florida schools, the Holocaust will to be taught across the curriculum with content infused in ways that are age-appropriate, interdisciplinary, and in every grade-level."*[10] *(The quote is as it was presented on the website of the Florida Department of Education.)*

According to the Jewish Virtual Library's website, in 2020 there were sixteen states that required schools to provide Holocaust education studies. They were California, Colorado, Connecticut, Delaware, Florida, Illinois, Indiana, Kentucky, Michigan, New Hampshire, New Jersey, New York, Oregon, Rhode Island, Texas, and Virginia. Additionally, states that were encouraging Holocaust education were Pennsylvania and Washington.

---

[10] Florida Department of Education. (n.d.). *Commissioner of Education's Task Force on Holocaust Education.* Retrieved December 28, 2021, from https://www.fldoe.org/holocausteducation/

Compare the emphasis on Holocaust instruction in our nation's schools to that of civics instruction. The disparity continues to widen between the two.

3. Censorship

Unfortunately, we live in a world of censorship. Opposing views are ridiculed and those espousing such views are subjected to ad hominem attacks. Indeed, this extends from social media comments to historical research. It is not surprising then, that persons have been punished for raising questions about the Holocaust.

At least sixteen European nations and Israel have laws which forbid Holocaust denial. In some of those countries, laws criminalize such denial.

In 2005, British author David Irving, was arrested for Holocaust denial in Austria. In 2006, he was convicted and sentenced to three years in prison. He served thirteen months after a reduction of his sentence. In 2017, a German Court sentenced an eighty-nine-year-old woman, Ursula Haverbeck, to serve two years in prison for Holocaust denial. Closer to home, a former school principal in Florida was fired in 2020

for alleged comments he had made regarding the Holocaust,

notwithstanding his assertion that he was not a Holocaust

denier.

4. Civics Instruction vs. Holocaust Studies

And who is the winner? The growing emphasis on

Holocaust instruction in our nation's schools in comparison to

the diminishing support for civics instruction appears to

underscore the contention that the Holocaust has become a

priority over civics.

According to an article in the American Educator, "A

Look at Civics Education in the United States", summer 2018

edition:

"Only nine states and the District of

Columbia require one year of U.S. government or

civics, whereas 30 states require a half-year and the

other 11 states have no civics requirement." [11]

---

[11] Shapiro, S. and Brown, C. (2018, Summer). *A Look at Civics Education in the United States*. American Educator. Retrieved December 28, 2021, from https://files.eric.ed.gov/fulltext/EJ1182087.pdf

Idaho, for its part, introduces civics instruction as early as kindergarten.

In Florida, Gov. Ron DeSantis has proposed a $3,000 bonus for Florida teachers, but only if they complete training and certification for what is called "the Florida civic seal of excellence," a new civics education program. DeSantis also wants high school graduates to pass a civics test similar to the one taken by aspiring U.S. citizens.

As I had written earlier, there were sixteen states that required schools to provide Holocaust education studies. Moreover, two additional states were giving consideration to the implementation of Holocaust instruction. It is only a matter of time, in my opinion, until Holocaust education becomes a nationwide mandate.

From our discussion, it appears that our schools for the most part are failing to give priority to civics instruction over Holocaust studies. Our children need to develop an understanding of how our government functions and their role in shaping our future. The future of our nation is dependent upon the ability of each generation to take up the torch that has been passed to it and carry forward the ideals of this land. By doing so, we may continue to serve as a beacon of hope and prosperity on the world stage. An uninformed and uninspired citizenry, however, will not be able to carry out their responsibilities to enable our nation to continue to remain strong and prosperous.

On the other hand, learning about the Holocaust can be taught in history class. Topics can be presented leading to discussions on the social upheavals and humanitarian suffering during WWII.

5. Other Victims of Atrocities

Why don't schools teach students about other atrocities that have been committed by totalitarian regimes against innocent people? There have been many throughout history. Briefly, let us examine some of those events.

Armenian Genocide

During World War I, approximately 1.2 million Armenians were slaughtered by the rulers of what was then known as the Ottoman Empire, present-day Republic of

Turkey. As of 2021, thirty nations, including the U.S., have recognized the events as genocide. Turkey, however, has denied its complicity in genocide against the Armenian people.

Holodomor

The Great Famine of Ukraine, popularly known as the Holodomor, was the forced starvation of Ukrainian people during 1932-1933 by the Soviet regime under Joseph Stalin. A United Nations joint statement signed by twenty-five nations in 2003 declared that between seven to ten million Ukrainians perished during that period. That is more than had perished during the Jewish Holocaust.

Rwanda

Rwanda is a landlocked nation in East-Central Africa. During the Rwandan Civil War in 1994, approximately 800,000 persons perished as a result of genocide between the warring factions.

Karen

The Karen are an ethnic group from Myanmar (formerly Burma) which is north of Thailand. The Karen have five known religions, including Christianity. They have been the victims of persecution in one of the longest-running civil wars in recorded history which continues into the twenty-first century. Many Karen refugees of the Christian faith reside in the U.S.

Karen is also a racist slur that is used to describe "privileged" White women in the U.S. There are even laws that have been written known as "Karen" laws or "Caren" laws making it a crime for a White women to call 911 if she feels threatened by a black person. If I were a Karen refugee, I would be most offended by the insensitive usage of Karen.

So, why do our public schools give scant attention to those atrocities in comparison to that of the Holocaust? Human life is sacred, regardless of whether that life is Jewish, Armenian, Ukrainian, Rwandan, Karen, or the lives of other people. *All lives matter!* If our public school officials and politicians will accept that premise, then Holocaust studies should be modified to incorporate other events that have led to human suffering and atrocities.

6. Black History

In 1977, the television miniseries *Roots* was aired on nationwide television in the U.S. The series was based on Alex Haley's novel of the same name. *Roots* is the story of Haley's family, beginning with his seventh-generation ancestor, Kunta Kinte, who was sold into the slave trade after being abducted from his African village and brought to the U.S. After the showing of *Roots* there was a strong interest in the study of black history.

The *Roots* miniseries preceded the *Holocaust* series by one year. What the *Diary of Anne Frank* and the *Holocaust* miniseries did for Holocaust studies, *Roots* did for black history. Our public schools began to emphasize Holocaust studies and black history in their curriculum. School budgets allocated precious taxpayer dollars to develop programs in those areas. The major victim of this shift in curriculum was civics education. There were precious few hours remaining in a school day and even fewer dollars in a school budget to be allocated to programs dedicated to the teaching of civics.

Priority was given to instruction in the Holocaust and in black history. On the other hand, civics instruction had lost its appeal.

7. Say Our Name

The blacks, who were involuntarily brought to the American colonies and later to the U.S. following the American Revolution, were called *nigger* or *nigga*. The term was derived from the region in which many of the slaves had been sold into slavery. It was the region in West Africa surrounding the Niger River. Upon their emancipation from slavery, however, it was no longer proper to refer to black people in such a pejorative sense but instead as *coloreds*. Indeed, by 1909, the National Association for the Advancement of Colored People (NAACP) was founded in New York City. In addition to *colored*, the term *negro* became common usage. In the 1960s, advocates of black power gave inspiration to the term *black* to refer to black Americans. Moreover, following the popularity of the television series

Roots, the black community began to identify with the term *African American*. That is where we are in this present day.

8. What Dat?

Initially, black history focused on achievements of black Americans. Studies on the slave trade and the establishment of slavery in America, however, led the proponents of black history to question western civilization. Additionally, Christianity, the founding fathers, our constitution, and the moral foundation of our nation were also subjected to criticism. The result was the "cancel culture" movement. It was no longer sufficient just to study the achievements of black Americans. There had to be an assault on the principles and values which form the bedrock of our nation. Therefore, concomitant with the promotion of "cancel culture" by its idealogues, there was the development of forced instruction in "critical race theory". Both "cancel culture" and "critical race theory" will be examined in depth in subsequent chapters.

9. LGBTQ

In addition to Holocaust studies and black history, the LGBTQ community has pressured our schools into developing a curriculum to support its agenda. LGBTQ is an acronym for lesbian, gay, bisexual, transgender, and queer (or questioning). It is used to describe a person's sexual orientation or gender.

Of all those categories of sexual orientation that I have listed, "transgender" is perhaps the most controversial of the group. Science tells us that we are born either male or female. Well, that is true, but there have been rare exceptions.

Sometimes nature becomes confused, however, and decides to play a joke on humans. Such as when a baby is born with two heads. Another example of nature's cruelty is when a person has been born with both male and female reproductive organs. In that case, the person is called a hermaphrodite. Robert Ripley's *Believe It or Not* had documented only one such case in human history.

Hermaphroditism is an extremely rare birth defect. Any further discussion of this abnormality, however, is complex and beyond the scope of this book. Therefore, let us agree that humans are born either male or female, except in exceedingly rare instances when nature deviates from its intended outcome.

What do transgender people claim is their gender? Male-born transgenders claim that although they were born male, there is a female inside of them waiting to escape their male body. Female-born transgenders claim just the opposite. This is nonsense. A person is born either male or female.

Why has gender become such an issue? Until recently, a person with an alternative lifestyle was either gay or lesbian. Men who dressed up as women were called transvestites but were still considered gay. A transgender person (transsexual), on the other hand, is one whose physical characteristics have been altered to bring them into alignment with their gender identity.

How did society view and deal with such persons prior to the judicial rulings that now protect their lifestyle? Here are a few anecdotes that may be of interest to the reader:

124

The gay principal. The year was 1956 and I was in sixth grade. One day, the principal of the school, an effeminate man, came into my classroom to address the class on some school matter. His presence stirred up quite a commotion. The scent he exuded as he walked about our rows of desks was a flowery scent, the kind of scent you would experience if you were surrounded by a few dozen roses. Comments, such as, "Wow, what is that after shave he is using?" rang out in the classroom. In addition, he was wearing a ruffled shirt with pink embroidery emblazoned over the garment. It was the kind of garment I would have expected to have been worn by one of my female classmates. Again, comments resonated throughout the classroom. "Man, what a wild looking shirt!" exclaimed one of my classmates. During the commotion, I happened to steal a glance at my classroom teacher, Miss Kenney. She was trying her best to refrain from bursting out in laughter at the scene. Her smile, however, belied her efforts.

Most of us attending sixth grade were eleven years old. Moreover, there was no cable television in 1956. Therefore, we had limited exposure to the various types of programming that children are exposed to today. Additionally, television networks and movie theaters followed strict guidance on the types of content that could be shown to its viewers. They contained no obscenities and no sex scenes. Furthermore, LGBTQ issues were never broached for discussion in school. Thus, it should come as no surprise, that we had little or no knowledge of the lifestyles of persons in the LGBTQ community. Those were the times.

Some years later, I had asked my mother what had happened to the principal of my elementary school. She informed me that he had been fired by the school board because he was gay. She added that I was too young to understand why he had been fired, so I was never apprised of the reason for his dismissal. Apparently, he had been fired to protect the children attending the elementary school from his immoral behavior. Would he be fired today?

In the Navy. By the time I was in high school, a classmate had told me about a friend of his who had been serving in the Navy. One weekend while on shore leave, the friend had picked up someone at a bar whom he had thought to be a woman but turned out to be a man in drag. The guy in drag or transvestite was severely beaten by the sailor. Sailors beware of counterfeits!

Queers not allowed. At a men's pub in Providence, RI, some friends and I were talking to Sam, a black male who had owned the bar. Suddenly, two guys walked into the pub and Sam politely asked them to leave the premises. "Sam", I inquired, "why did you ask them to leave?" Sam responded mockingly, "I'd rather serve niggers than queers!"

Screwy Louie. Unbeknownst to me, the town in which I had begun my teaching career had its own resident transvestite. One of my students, Sara, had told me about a certain person she and her mother had met while shopping for groceries. She told me that her mother was puzzled as to the gender of the person. Sara added, "I told her that it was Screwy Louie. He's a guy who likes to dress up as a woman." Sara further explained that "Screwy Louie" was the name given to that character by the kids in town.

The doctor is out of the office. How are transvestites treated by the medical profession? A nurse I had been dating,

Gail, worked at a teaching-hospital in Boston. According to Gail, male doctors wanted nothing to do with guys in drag and would avoid them as much as possible, unless in an extreme emergency. Instead, the nurses would attend to their care.

In its quest to gain acceptance in society and equal treatment under the law, the LGBTQ community has found allies in the teachers' unions, halls of congress, judicial system, and Hollywood. Although the teachers' unions have become advocates for the LGBTQ agenda, a distinction needs to be made between how the teachers' unions operate and how individual teachers view their responsibilities. This may come as a surprise, but most teachers seldom endorse their unions initiatives. That is true when it comes to LGBTQ indoctrination of children in our public schools. Unfortunately, teachers are often coerced into supporting an agenda for fear of losing their jobs.

As of 2020, there were four states that mandated teaching LGBTQ history. Those states were California, Colorado, Illinois, and New Jersey. That list is expected to grow in subsequent years.

Children in public schools are being indoctrinated into believing that the new normal standard of sexual behavior includes persons who identify as LGBTQ. Some of the prevailing topics of discussion found in public schools are: "it's okay to be gay", "mommy's got a girlfriend", and "daddy's got a boyfriend". There are several problems with that type of instruction. One, children are not at a level of maturity that they can make decisions on sexual and gender identity. This is especially true for children at the lower grade levels. On the other hand, students in high school are at a level of maturity where they can better understand the complexities of human nature. Two, LGBTQ instruction may contravene a child's moral upbringing, religious beliefs, and values. Strong family values are important in a child's development. Three, society still embraces traditional norms. That conflicts with the LGBTQ lifestyle.

What is the position of our judicial system on LGBTQ rights? In its landmark case, Obergefell v. Hodges (2015), the U.S. Supreme Court in a 5-4 decision upheld same-sex marriages. It ruled that the Fourteenth Amendment required all states to grant same-sex marriages and recognize same-sex marriages that were granted in other states.

However, the U.S. Supreme Court ruled in a 7-2 decision in Masterpiece Cakeshop v. Colorado Civil Rights Commission (2018) that a Colorado baker could not be forced to make a cake for a same sex couple's wedding. The Court stated that the legal proceedings in Colorado had been hostile to the baker's religious views. The verdict was viewed as a victory for religious freedom under the First Amendment. LGBTQ proponents, however, were not impressed with the ruling.

On the other hand, in a 6-3 decision, the Supreme Court ruled in Bostock v. Clayton County (2020) that under Title VII of the Civil Rights Act of 1964, which protects employees against discrimination because they are gay or transgender, the term "sex" includes a person's sexual orientation and gender identity. In layman's language it means that an employer cannot refuse to hire or fire somebody because they are gay or transgender.

How has our military responded to the LGBTQ community? On or about September 20, 2011, the military repealed its "don't ask, don't tell" policy. Furthermore, it repealed its transgender ban on or about January 25, 2021.

Congress, on the other hand, has been slow in approving legislation in support of LGBTQ rights. The present Congress would like nothing more than to expand those rights. There is pending legislation that would do just that, however, it is being stalled because of a lack of bipartisan support.

10. Old Glory vs. LGBTQ Banner

In a 5-4 decision, the Supreme Court Ruled in Texas v. Johnson (1989) that the burning of the U.S. flag is a protected form of free speech under the First Amendment. Woe to anybody, however, who dares to burn an LGBTQ banner.

According to the Des Moines Register, an Iowa man was sentenced to sixteen years in prison in 2019 for having the audacity to remove a LGBTQ banner from an alternative lifestyle church and set it on fire. Moreover, he was the first person to be convicted of a hate crime in the Iowa county.

Justifiably, there were online posts that protested the sentence. People were appalled that a person could burn the flag of the U.S. with impunity but face imprisonment for setting fire to a gay banner.

Interestingly, the same church two years earlier sponsored a Halloween party for its youth. It was called "Drag-O-Ween" to signal its inclusiveness.

11. Anti-Bullying Rules

Do you remember the schoolyard bully? He (or she) was someone who had the body of an adult but the mind of a child. In addition, they loved to throw their weight around, both literally and figuratively.

Moreover, before schools had adopted the policy of social promotion to advance a student from one grade level to the next grade level, it was not uncommon to find sixteen-year-olds sitting in classrooms with eleven-year-olds. That was the case when I had attended school. It also created an environment that encouraged bullying.

What actions did teachers take to discourage bullying in school? Teachers, with exceptions, would generally look the other way.

Bullying is still a problem in our nation's schools. According to students with whom I have spoken, teachers continue to turn their heads and look the other way rather than confront the school bullies.

There is one exception. That exception is the LGBTQ community. Schools have now adopted "anti-bullying" rules to protect the gay students from school bullying. On the other hand, students who are not gay continue to be denied protection from bullies by school authorities.

12. Demise of Civics Instruction

We will now return to the question that was proposed at the beginning of this chapter's discussion, "Where Has Civics Instruction Gone?" As Holocaust studies, black history, and LGBTQ instruction continue to be emphasized in our nation's schools, there has been a marked decline in support for civics instruction. School budgets and class time are limited resources that must be allocated among competing disciplines.

Unfortunately, civics instruction is no longer of paramount

importance in the education of our children. Parents need to

demand that their school boards return to providing the

resources for civics instruction in their schools.

Chapter Seven

Cancel Culture

1. War on American Values

As he gave the order to burn Rome, the Roman Emperor Nero allegedly had said, "In order to create, I must first destroy." One of his key advisers, the philosopher Seneca, imploringly asked, "But your Majesty, to destroy all the historical monuments, buildings, and cultural works of Rome, a Rome though imperfect, is it wise to do so?" Seneca's admonishment of Nero should be a warning to those who wish to rewrite our history and replace our culture.

In 2020, we were confronted by the actions of certain individuals and groups whose purpose has been to remake our nation. Their goal is to "cancel our culture". Thus, Merriam-Webster has a new term to add to its lexicon, namely, *cancel culture*.

The big question is, why? Why cancel our culture and heritage? The answer lies in part in the movement that has embraced the transition from nation states to a more global world order. World War II has been viewed by many as having been an unnecessary evil brought about by nationalism (or patriotism). *Nationalism*, according to Merriam-Webster, is "...loyalty and devotion to a nation... a sense of national consciousness... exalting one nation above all others and placing primary emphasis on promotion of its culture and interests as opposed to those of other nations...." The opposite of nationalism is internationalism or globalization. Those who adhere to the latter doctrine believe that wars, poverty, and social injustice may be eliminated by rendering obsolete such concepts as nationalism. Moreover, they believe that we should think of ourselves as citizens of the world and not citizens of a particular nation.

A nation can be defined as one that has *borders, language, and culture*. Without borders, a common language, and a distinctly unique culture, there can be no nation. By eliminating a nation's borders, common language, and culture it will cease to be a nation.

What is happening in our nation today underscores an effort to eliminate our borders, common language, national heritage and culture. Until recently, our borders had been proven ineffective to control *illegal immigration*. If there is a return to failed immigration policies of the past, *illegal immigration* will increase precipitously, and our nightmares will become a reality.

Our common language, English, is under attack. The other day, I had received my billing statement for health insurance on two sheets of paper. One sheet, the actual bill, contained the amount of monthly premium. The other sheet (both sides) contained information that was written in at least two dozen languages. It was all Greek to me (satirical wit)! Will English continue as our national language?

As for our national culture and heritage, we have witnessed the wanton destruction of property, including the loss of lives, that have taken place nationwide in 2020. There have been calls to abolish Independence Day, Thanksgiving Day, and Columbus Day. There has been contempt displayed for the national anthem. In some cases, something called a "black national anthem" has been played at sporting events. Is there such a thing as a "black anthem"? Nations have anthems.

Since there is no black nation that exists in the U. S., how can a "black anthem" supplant our beloved national anthem?

The American flag has been burned on numerous occasions and there have been no penalties for such transgressions. However, a man in Iowa was sentenced to sixteen years in prison in December 2019 for having burned a LGBTQ pride flag. What a horrible message to send to our youth! Burn the Stars and Stripes with utmost impunity, but destroy other symbols of dubious value, only to face years of incarceration.

2. National Symbols of the United States

Our nation has several national symbols. Those symbols help identify who we are as a nation and as a people. Similarly, our states have certain symbols which distinguish them from each other. For example, "Live Free or Die" is the official motto of New Hampshire. On the other hand, "Salus Populi Suprema Lex Esto" is the Missouri state motto. It is Latin and translates to, "let the welfare of the people be the supreme law". Therefore, just as each state has its own symbols, the U. S. has adopted its own symbols. Let's examine some of our national symbols and their importance to us as a people.

Our flag, often referred to as "Old Glory" and "The Stars and Stripes", is our "colors". It gives us a common identity and a sense of belonging to a culture that is uniquely American. The protagonists of cancel culture have declared war on our national flag. A separate section herein will be devoted to discussing their attacks on our flag.

Our national anthem is "The Star-Spangled Banner". Similar to our national flag, it is also under attack by those who wish to cancel our culture. The assault on our national anthem will be addressed in our discussion of the denigration of our flag.

The official seal of our nation is referred to as "The Great Seal of the United States". The Great Seal of the United States was first introduced in 1782. It is used to authenticate certain documents that are issued by the federal government. The Great Seal has two sides. Beginning in 1935, both sides of the Great Seal have appeared on the reverse side of the one-dollar bill.

On the front (or obverse) of the Great Seal is the coat of arms of the U.S. It is this side of the Seal with which most people are familiar. In the center of the Seal is the bald eagle. Above its head are 13 stars, signifying the number of original states and the motto, *E Pluribus Unum* (meaning "out of many, one"). Furthermore, the eagle is holding an olive branch in its right talon and 13 arrows in its left talon. Together they symbolize that the U.S. has a desire for peace but it will always be ready for war. In Latin there is an adage, *"Si vis pacem, para bellum"* which translates to "if you want peace, prepare for war."

Great Seal of the U.S. (obverse).
Wikimedia Commons. Author: U.S. Government.
Public Domain.

On the reverse of the Great Seal are symbols that have their origin in Freemasonry. There is an unfinished pyramid. Above the pyramid, is an eye in a triangle. Additionally, two mottos appear above and below the pyramid. One, appearing above the pyramid, *Annuit Coeptis*, indicates that a higher power "looks with favor on our undertakings". Two, *Novus Ordo Seclorum* meaning "a new order of the ages" sits below the pyramid. At the base of the pyramid are Roman numerals signifying "1776" or the year of independence of the U.S.

Great Seal of the U.S. (reverse).
Wikimedia Commons. Author: Ipankonin.

The reverse of the $1 bill. Photo by Robert V. Carabina.

The national bird of the U.S. is the bald eagle. The bald eagle appears on our Great Seal and on our currency.

Our national motto is officially, "In God We Trust." Our unofficial motto is *E Pluribus Unum* which is Latin for "out of many, one". It signifies that as thirteen original states we are now one united nation. In addition, it may be interpreted as meaning, from many cultures we are now one culture, American.

3. The Flag and The Star-Spangled Banner

Our national flag and our national anthem have become the two most vilified symbols of our national culture by those who desire to destroy our national heritage. Those political antagonists do not possess a clear understanding of what those symbols mean to us as a people and to our nation.

The flag represents the sharing of a common set of values and beliefs. In addition, it means belonging to a group which embraces those values and beliefs.

Before there were nations, families distinguished themselves with family crests and coat of arms. When the Knight Templars fought the Muslims for control of the Holy Land, they carried with them into battle the cross, emblazoned on their shields or held on high by a standard-bearer. Over the centuries, armies have gone into battle with a flag-bearer carrying the flag of their nation.

143

Having a flag-bearer holding the flag on high served several purposes. One, if soldiers were separated from their main unit, they would be able to rejoin it, if they could spot their nation's flag from a distance. Two, affixing the flag on a structure, or on a pole and planting it in the ground, would signal to soldiers in the field that the objective of the battle had been a success. Three, the flag served as a morale booster. If the flag could be seen by soldiers in battle, it inspired them to continue fighting the enemy.

During the war of 1812, Francis Scott Key authored the poem, "Defense of Fort McHenry", which was later renamed, "The Star-Spangled Banner". The poem was written on the back of an old letter. Key was inspired to write the poem after he stood in awe and witnessed the raising of the garrison flag (American flag) at Fort McHenry on September 14, 1814. That day held special significance because Fort McHenry was under heavy bombardment by the British. The British failed, however, in taking the fort. The raising of the flag signified that the American garrison had held the fort and had repelled the onslaught by the British.

Key was on a British warship during the siege of Fort McHenry. He was being detained after he had won the release of a friend from the ship's prison. One can only imagine the excitement that overcame him as he stood on that British vessel and viewed the raising of the flag at Fort McHenry.

Of what importance was Fort McHenry, that the British attacked the compound? The British had already sacked Washington City. They had burned the Capitol and other buildings. In addition, they had set the White House on fire. Their next stop was Baltimore, a vital seaport. Fort McHenry, however, guarded Baltimore's inner harbor and remained an obstacle in the path of the British on their way into Baltimore. The failure of the British to take the fort prevented them from advancing into Baltimore.

There were 1,000 Americans at Fort McHenry under the command of Major George Armistead. Heavy rain and high humidity accompanied the bombardment of the fort by the British. There were two flags at the fort. One was called a storm flag and measured 17 x 25 feet. It was smaller than the larger garrison flag (American flag) which had measured 30 x

42 feet. The larger garrison flag had been ordered by Major Armistead a year earlier from Mary Pickersgill, a local flag maker. Armistead commissioned the larger garrison flag because he wanted a flag "so large that the British will have no difficulty in seeing it from a distance." The garrison flag was the one that was raised every morning at reveille. It is the flag believed to have been seen by Francis Scott Key on the morning of September 14, 1814. For those interested, the flag can be seen on display at the Smithsonian Institution. The smaller storm flag has been lost forever to history.

There were local accounts that during the bombardment of the fort, the storm flag had fallen and the dead bodies of Americans were used to prop the flag up so that it could be seen from a distance. In actuality, the pole on which the flag had been fastened had become bent and American soldiers reset it to make sure it could still be seen flying above the fort. Those soldiers understood the importance of their actions and the significance of having the flag seen flying above the fort.

Perhaps the most iconic wartime photograph of the American flag being raised in battle occurred on the Japanese island of Iwo Jima in the Pacific during World War II. During the waning months of the war in 1945, U.S. Marines engaged the Japanese Army in one of the fiercest military campaigns in the Pacific, the Battle of Iwo Jima. Iwo Jima lay some 750 miles off the coast of mainland Japan. The battle lasted approximately five weeks. The Japanese were heavily outnumbered. Marines outnumbered the Japanese approximately 70,000 to 21,000. Reports indicated that 7,000 Marines were killed and approximately 25,000 casualties were recorded in the battle. Except for an estimated 200 survivors, all other Japanese were killed in battle on the island. Even after their defeat, several remaining Japanese soldiers refused to surrender and hid in the jungles attempting to evade capture by American forces. It took several weeks of trudging through the jungles before Marines could capture or kill the remaining holdouts. Remarkably, two Japanese holdouts evaded capture by hiding out in caves on the island and finally surrendered in 1949, four years after the end of the war.

The Marines captured Mount Suribachi on the south side of Iwo Jima. The iconic photo of American Marines raising the flag on Iwo Jima was taken at the summit on Suribachi. What a lot of people do not realize is that the raising of the flag had occurred four days into the fighting. The battle would rage on for another four weeks on the northern side of Iwo Jima. The raising of the flag, however, was an inspiration to the Marines and propelled them to eventual victory.

Marines raising the American Flag on Mount Suribachi on the island of Iwo Jima during World War II. This was the second flag-raising on top of Mount Suribachi and was taken by Joe Rosenthal on or about February 23, 1945. The Associated Press has relinquished its copyright to the photograph allowing it to be placed in the public domain.

"The Star-Spangled Banner" is the national anthem of the U.S. As I had stated earlier, it was written by Francis Scott Key. The poem was set to the tune of a British song, however, that had been written by John Stafford Smith for the Anacreontic Society, which was a men's social club in London, England. It was officially adopted as the nation's national anthem by a congressional resolution and signed into law by President Herbert Hoover in 1931. There are four stanzas to the national anthem. The first stanza is the one with which Americans are most familiar and is sung at events. Here are those lyrics to our national anthem as written by Francis Scott Key with original spelling and punctuation:

O say can you see, by the dawn's early light,

What so proudly we hail'd at the twilight's last gleaming,

Whose broad stripes and bright stars through the perilous fight

O'er the ramparts we watch'd were so gallantly streaming?

And the rocket's red glare, the bomb bursting in air,

Gave proof through the night that our flag was still there,

O say does that star-spangled banner yet wave

O'er the land of the free and the home of the brave?

On the shore dimly seen through the mists of the deep

Where the foe's haughty host in dread silence reposes,

What is that which the breeze, o'er the towering steep,

As it fitfully blows, half conceals, half discloses?

Now it catches the gleam of the morning's first beam,

In full glory reflected now shines in the stream,

'Tis the star-spangled banner - O long may it wave

O'er the land of the free and the home of the brave!

And where is that band who so vauntingly swore,

That the havoc of war and the battle's confusion

A home and a Country should leave us no more?

Their blood has wash'd out their foul footstep's pollution.

No refuge could save the hireling and slave

From the terror of flight or the gloom of the grave,

And the star-spangled banner in triumph doth wave

O'er the land of the free and the home of the brave.

O thus be it ever when freemen shall stand

Between their lov'd home and the war's desolation!

Blest with vict'ry and peace may the heav'n rescued land

Praise the power that hath made and preserv'd us a nation!

Then conquer we must, when our cause it is just,

And this be our motto - "In God is our trust,"

And the star-spangled banner in triumph shall wave

O'er the land of the free and the home of the brave.[12]

---

[12] National Museum of American History. (n.d.). *Complete version of 'The Star-Spangled Banner showing spelling and punctuation from Francis Scott Key's manuscript in the Maryland Historical Society collection.* Smithsonian Institute. Retrieved October 18, 2021, from https://amhistory.si.edu/starspangledbanner/pdf/ssb_lyrics.pdf

Prior to "The Star-Spangled Banner" becoming our national anthem in 1931, there were other songs that were played at national events and which had served as our national anthem. In the early days of the Republic, "Hail Columbia", initially called "The President's March", was one such song. Its music was composed in 1789 and the lyrics to the song were written in 1798.

"America (My Country Tis of Thee)" was written in 1831 and became our de facto national anthem. Then, in 1893 "America the Beautiful" became a popular national song. Notwithstanding strong support for "America the Beautiful", it was finally decided in 1931 that "The Star-Spangled Banner" would be our national anthem.

Brave Americans have sacrificed their lives over the years in countless battles to preserve our flag and what it represents so that succeeding generations will understand its significance to our national heritage. Just as a torch is passed from one person to the next person, each new generation of Americans should preserve for the next generation of

Americans the legacy of our flag and its significance to our national consciousness.

When professional athletes take a knee to the playing of the national anthem and the flying of our nation's flag, it undermines the sacrifices of all those Americans who have fought and died to preserve our nation. Moreover, when sporting events are conducted in another nation and American athletes stand for that nation's anthem but then kneel when the American anthem is played, they display their lack of respect for our nation's values. What a disgrace! No athlete from another nation would display such total disrespect to their nation's heritage, as those American athletes have exhibited towards our nation's heritage.

In 2007, the U.S. Congress addressed etiquette for the Pledge of Allegiance and the national anthem in 36 USC 301. When the flag passes by, such as in a parade, or when reciting the Pledge of Allegiance, one should stand at attention, face the flag, and salute by placing the right hand over the heart. In the case of armed forces personnel, firefighters, and law enforcement officers, it is proper to present the military salute.

Patrons attending a sporting event should rise, stand at attention, and salute by placing their right hand over their heart at the playing of The Star-Spangled Banner.

When I had attended school, students were given instructions in etiquette for our flag, reciting the Pledge of Allegiance, and the playing of The Star-Spangled Banner. Unfortunately, that appears to have become a lost practice in our public schools.

4. 1776 or 1619

The Spirit of '76. On July 4, 1776, the Second Continental Congress met and unanimously adopted the Declaration of Independence, which proclaimed the American colonies' separation from England. From that day forward, the colonies would be free and independent from the British yoke. Henceforth, they would operate as an independent republic founded upon democratic principles.

Each year we celebrate July 4 as our Independence Day. As a youngster, I was awed by the fireworks display that took place on that day in my hometown. As a history teacher, one of my most memorable class projects was to create a time capsule with my students in 1976, the 200th anniversary of our nation's independence. Even today, I still get a thrill watching firework displays on July 4.

The following passage from the Declaration of Independence reads as follows:

> *We hold these truths to be self-evident, that all men are created equal, that they are endowed by their Creator with certain unalienable Rights, that among these are Life, Liberty and the pursuit of Happiness.--That to secure these rights, Governments are instituted among Men, deriving their just powers from the consent of the governed, --That whenever any Form of Government becomes destructive of these ends, it is the Right of the People to alter or to abolish it, and to institute new Government, laying its foundation on such principles and organizing its powers in such form, as to them shall seem most likely to effect their Safety and Happiness.* [13]

---

[13] America's Founding Documents. (n.d.). *Declaration of Independence: A Transcription.* National Archives. Retrieved December 30,2021, from https://www.archives.gov/founding-docs/declaration-transcript

If the passage sounds familiar, it should be familiar since it is read in U.S. history classes throughout our nation. Or should I say, it used to be once upon a time. As a student, I had to memorize that passage from the Declaration of Independence.

Unfortunately, those who wish to denigrate our nation and its values by cancelling our culture, do not hold those words in high esteem. Are we going to allow the voices of destruction and chaos to poison the minds of future generations by their vilification of that document and the maligning of its authors?

A former professional athlete, one of the voices of chaos and destruction, wrote this on his "Twitter" account on July 4, 2020:

Black ppl have been dehumanized, brutalized, criminalized + terrorized by America for centuries, & are expected to join your commemoration of "independence", while you enslaved our ancestors.

We reject your celebration of white supremacy &

look forward to liberation for all.[14]

Now that clearly is a person who should not be allowed within shouting distance of a public school classroom. Perhaps he needs to apply for a library card to familiarize himself with the history of the founding of our nation. He would then understand the significance of documents such as the Declaration of Independence and the Constitution.

1619 Project. In 2019, the 1619 Project began as an attempt by radical journalists and The New York Times to commemorate the 400th anniversary of the arrival of some twenty captive Africans in the English colony of Virginia. As the story goes, they were allegedly brought to America aboard a Dutch ship after having been captured by a joint African-Portuguese raid in modern-day Angola. The project attempts to reexamine the history of slavery in the U.S. and uses 1619 as the starting point in its timeline.

---

[14] Linder, B. (2020, July 4). *Colin Kaepernick rips Fourth of July as 'celebration of white supremacy' on Twitter.* Penn Live. Retrieved December 30, 2021, from https://www.pennlive.com/sports/2020/07/colin-kaepernick-rips-fourth-of-july-as-celebration-of-white-supremacy-on-twitter.html

Prominent historians have taken issue with the project

for some of its outlandish claims. For instance, Nikole Hannah-

Jones, one of the developers of the project, makes the

unsupported claim that, "one of the primary reasons the

colonists decided to declare their independence from Britain

was because they wanted to protect the institution of slavery".[15]

In addition, Abraham Lincoln is portrayed as a "white

supremacist" by the project developers.

The authors of the project have sought to replace

historical fact with unsupported fictional claims. Furthermore,

they have envisioned the development of a curriculum to be

used in public schools which would effectively rewrite the

history of the U.S. Will this propaganda be permitted to be

taught to our children and future generations of Americans?

President Donald Trump had attempted to put the

brakes on the radicals' pursuit of their agenda. As a response to

the 1619 Project, he issued an executive order establishing the

---

[15] Serwer, A. (2019, December 23). *The Fight Over the 1619 Project Is Not About the Facts.* The Atlantic. Retrieved December 30, 2021, from https://www.theatlantic.com/ideas/archive/2019/12/historians-clash-1619-project/604093/

1776 Commission in September 2020. The aim of the commission was to support "patriotic education" in our schools. To that end, the commission released a report on January 18, 2021. The following statement appeared on the website trumpwhitehouse.archives.gov directing readers to a link to view and print a copy of that report:

1776 Commission—comprised of some of America's most distinguished scholars and historians—has released a report presenting a definitive chronicle of the American founding, a powerful description of the effect the principles of the Declaration of Independence have had on this Nation's history, and a dispositive rebuttal of reckless "re-education" attempts that seek to reframe American history around the idea that the United States is not an exceptional country but an evil one.[16]

Two days after the release of the report, newly elected President Joseph Biden, on January 20, 2021, terminated the

---

[16] Trump Whitehouse. (2021, January 18). *1776 Commission Takes Historic and Scholarly Step to Restore Understanding of the Greatness of the American Founding.* Retrieved December 30, 2021, from https://trumpwhitehouse.archives.gov/briefings-statements/1776-commission-takes-historic-scholarly-step-restore-understanding-greatness-american-founding/

1776 Commission by executive order. Biden placed the wishes

of radical journalists, supporters of Black Lives Matter, and the

teachers' unions ahead of the good of our nation. In addition,

his executive order did irreparable damage to our schools and

to our children.

5. Thanksgiving Day

One of my favorite holidays is Thanksgiving. It is a

time for families to gather around a table to partake of a

sumptuous feast and give thanks to the Lord for having

provided us with such a bounty of provisions. As a youngster, I

recall Thanksgiving Day dinner, courtesy of my mother and

grandmother. The dinner consisted of a large turkey, stuffing,

mashed potatoes, sweet potatoes, gravy, squash, cranberry

sauce, biscuits, pumpkin, and apple pies.

In addition, there was the traditional Macy's

Thanksgiving Day parade followed by the long-established

NFL football game. The Detroit Lions hosted those games

beginning in 1934 and, with the exception of World War II,

have continued in that tradition to this day. Furthermore, in

1966, the Dallas Cowboys were approved to host a game on

Thanksgiving Day. This provided football fans with an NFL

doubleheader, the Lions being featured in the early game and

the Cowboys in the later game.

Notwithstanding our national tradition, along came the

party-poopers. They are the ones who believe that to celebrate

Thanksgiving is to celebrate "genocide". The genocide of

indigenous people. They want to replace Thanksgiving Day

with a "National Day of Mourning".

It was President George Washington, in his first term as

president of the U.S., who had called for an official day of

thanksgiving and prayer. The holiday, however, did not

become an annual event until President Abraham Lincoln

issued a proclamation establishing the last Thursday of

November as Thanksgiving Day on October 3, 1863. Lincoln

issued this declaration during the Civil War to give praise to

God for the "fruitful fields"[17] bestowed to us and "… to heal

---

[17] Collected Works of Abraham Lincoln. (n.d.). *Proclamation of Thanksgiving*. Abraham Lincoln Online. Retrieved December 30, 2021, from http://www.abrahamlincolnonline.org/lincoln/speeches/thanks.htm

the wounds of the nation and to restore it as soon as may be consistent with the Divine purposes to the full enjoyment of peace, harmony, tranquility and Union."[18] President Franklin Delano Roosevelt in 1939, however, moved the holiday to the next to the last Thursday in November for the period 1939-1941. He did so, presumably, to boost the economy by providing both shoppers and merchants an extra week to conduct business between Thanksgiving and Christmas. Congress, however, had other ideas. In 1941, Roosevelt agreed at the behest of Congress, to restore Thanksgiving to the last Thursday in November, effective with the year 1942. That permanently established the official day of Thanksgiving.

Despite all the acrimony denouncing Thanksgiving Day by some misguided and uninformed iconoclasts, it remains a national holiday. Attempts by the advocates of "cancel culture" to eliminate Thanksgiving Day have made a lot of noise but the holiday remains a part of our national heritage. Thanksgiving is about families offering thanks to God for His blessings upon us

---

[18] Ibid.

and our nation. It is a tradition that needs to be passed along from one generation to the next generation. Will we be up to this task or will we allow the advocates of "cancel culture" to pursue an indoctrination of our children with a nihilistic doctrine that has as its goal social upheaval and a rewriting of our nation's history?

6. Andy Jackson or Auntie

In another instance of "cancel culture", Jack Lew, Treasury Secretary under President Barack Obama, in April of 2016, officially announced that former President and Freemason, Andrew Jackson, would be replaced by Harriet Tubman on the front of the $20 bill, with Jackson appearing on the reverse. However, a funny thing happened on the way to the engraving office. In the 2016 election, Donald Trump was elected President and the reissuance of the $20 bill has been delayed along with its accompanying changes.

Here is what the front of a new $20 bill would presumably look like with Harriet Tubman on the face of the bill:

Conceptual prototype of $20 bill prepared by the Bureau of Engraving and Printing. Digital editing of government image by Tim Davenport ("Carrite") for Wikipedia. No copyright claimed for the work. File released to the public domain without restriction.

7. Mount Rushmore

One of our most revered works of sculptural art, Mount Rushmore, is located in the Black Hills of South Dakota. It features the busts of former Presidents George Washington, Thomas Jefferson, Abraham Lincoln, and Teddy Roosevelt. Washington, Roosevelt and arguably Jefferson were Freemasons. The lead sculptor of the Rushmore monument was Gutzon Borglum. He also was involved, initially, in the Stone Mountain project in Georgia, but because of a dispute left it to others to complete the task. Borglum was a Freemason and an active member of Howard Lodge #35 in New York. Additionally, he had served as its Worshipful Master.

Mount Rushmore is considered a national treasure. It is a testament to the greatness of our nation. Yet, there are nefarious forces, who if they had their way, would reduce the

monument to rubble. Are we going to allow our greatest

national treasure to suffer this fate?

8. Juneteenth

Those who wish to cancel our culture contend that

contrary to popular belief, it was June 19, 1865 that marked the

end of slavery in the U.S., when remaining slaves were finally

freed in Texas. They are vociferous in their claim that the

issuance of the Emancipation Proclamation by President

Abraham Lincoln was an empty gesture to free the

slaves. Moreover, they want June 19 to be celebrated as a

national holiday and called Juneteenth. Should we to accept

this scurrilous claim as a pretext to rewriting our nation's

history? Incredibly, June 19 officially became a federal holiday

in the U.S. in June 2021. The holiday is called Juneteenth, the

blending of June and Nineteenth. Among black people, it is

their day of independence.

9. Teddy Roosevelt

Teddy Roosevelt was our twenty-sixth president. In addition, he was a former Rough Rider and distinguished Freemason. His sculptured bust lies alongside those of George Washington, Thomas Jefferson, and Abraham Lincoln on Mount Rushmore.

Roosevelt distinguished himself during the Spanish-American War when he and Leonard Wood in 1898 organized the 1st United States Volunteer Cavalry. Nicknamed the "Rough Riders", Roosevelt recruited a diverse group including cowboys, miners, law enforcement officials, and Native Americans to join the group. The Rough Riders are known for their heroic charge up San Juan Hill to help the U.S. secure an important strategic location near Santiago, Cuba. A few days after the volunteer regiment took San Juan Hill, the Spanish Fleet fled Cuba. A few weeks later the war ended, and the U.S. proclaimed victory.

Not surprisingly, Teddy Roosevelt was one of the most popular presidents in American history. On October 27, 1940, a statue of Roosevelt was erected in front of the American Museum of Natural History in New York City.

The sculpture, created by James Earle Fraser was cast by the Gorham Manufacturing Company in Providence, RI. It portrays Roosevelt on horseback flanked by a Native American and a person of African descent. According to Fraser, the work was intended to underscore Roosevelt's friendliness to all races.

The dissidents of cancel culture, however, called the statue a symbol of racism and colonialism. As a result of the pressure exerted by the counterculture element, the statue of Teddy Roosevelt has been designated to be removed from the front of the American Museum of Natural History. What is especially disconcerting is that Roosevelt's father was one of the founders of the museum. Moreover, Teddy Roosevelt donated many "trophies" from his hunts in Africa to the museum. As of the date of this writing, no information has been provided as to the new home for the Roosevelt statue.

What is truly appalling is the treatment given to the legacy of Teddy Roosevelt by those who wish to undermine his accomplishments. Roosevelt's memory is being tarnished as if he were an American pariah. Furthermore, those who wish to paint a picture of Roosevelt as a racist demonstrate their ignorance of U.S. history.

Compare the treatment of Roosevelt's memory to the treatment of the memory of a black felon named George Floyd. While Roosevelt's statue was being designated for relocation, statues of George Floyd were unveiled in New York and in New Jersey to commemorate Juneteenth. One statue, a bust of Floyd was on display in Brooklyn's Flatbush Junction. It was to remain there for approximately three weeks and then moved to Union Square in Manhattan. In addition, a seven-hundred-pound statue of Floyd was unveiled in front of City Hall in Newark. It was slated to remain there for at least one year.

What has happened to our nation when a black felon is hailed as a national hero and a true national hero is assigned to the dustbin of history? Wake up America!

10. Christopher Columbus

October 12, Columbus Day, is a federal holiday in the U.S. In addition, most states continue to observe Columbus Day. There has been a growing disdain of Columbus by those who wish to cancel our culture, however, and as a result Columbus Day has been replaced by Indigenous People's Day in several jurisdictions in the U.S. What has given rise to this development?

In observance of Columbus Day, students in elementary school once read a poem titled, *In 1492*, by Jean Marzollo:

In fourteen hundred ninety-two
Columbus sailed the ocean blue.

He had three ships and left from Spain;
He sailed through sunshine, wind and rain.

He sailed by night; he sailed by day;
He used the stars to find his way.

A compass also helped him know
How to find the way to go.

Ninety sailors were on board;
Some men worked while others snored.

Then the workers went to sleep;
And others watched the ocean deep.

Day after day they looked for land;
They dreamed of trees and rocks and sand.

October 12 their dream came true,
You never saw a happier crew!

"Indians! Indians!" Columbus cried;
His heart was filled with joyful pride.

But "India" the land was not;
It was the Bahamas, and it was hot.

The Arakawa natives were very nice;
They gave the sailors food and spice.

Columbus sailed on to find some gold
To bring back home, as he'd been told.

He made the trip again and again,
Trading gold to bring to Spain.

The first American? No, not quite.
But Columbus was brave, and he was bright.

How many students in our schools today will recite this poem in observance of Columbus Day? Moreover, how many of their teachers have ever read the poem?

Let us briefly examine the life of Christopher Columbus and perhaps gain some insight into why he is despised by the cancel culture mob. Columbus was born in Genoa, the capital city of the Republic of Genoa. His long ambition was to discover a direct water route to Asia by sailing west from Europe. Initially, Columbus approached the Portuguese king to finance his expedition, but the king turned down his request.

Next, he went to his native land, Genoa, and was similarly denied any financial support. The Republic of Venice was his next stop but there was little enthusiasm for his plan among the Venetians. Finally, he went to visit the Spanish Monarchy of Queen Isabella of Castile and Ferdinand II of Aragon who agreed to finance his voyages.

King Ferdinand and Queen Isabella had decided to provide Columbus with the financial support he had requested in the hope of finding riches in Asia. Additionally, they had hoped that a successful voyage by Columbus would catapult Spain to a prominent power among European nations. Embarking from Spain, Columbus made four trips across the Atlantic. His first voyage in 1492 was the most famous one. It was followed by voyages in 1493, 1498, and 1502.

On October 12, 1492, sailors had spotted land. Believing he had reached the Indian Ocean, Columbus thought he had found the East Indies. Therefore, he called the natives "Indians". However, Columbus was in the Caribbean Sea and had landed in the Americas, specifically the Bahamas.

It was Amerigo Vespucci, who in 1502, had determined that Columbus had discovered a new land. America was later named for Amerigo Vespucci.

After his third voyage to the "new world" Columbus was arrested and imprisoned for alleged administrative misconduct. Additionally, he was accused of employing harsh policies to govern the land he had named Hispaniola ("Little Spain"). Today, both the Dominican Republic and Haiti share the island of Hispaniola. Fortunately for Columbus, King Ferdinand personally intervened on his behalf and had him freed from prison.

There are conflicting accounts as to the discoverer of America. Some historians believe that other explorers had arrived in the Americas prior to Columbus. One person whose name regularly pops up is Leif Erikson, a Norse explorer from Iceland. He is believed to have been the first known European explorer to have set foot on the continent of North America. That is believed to have been around 1000 A.D., some five hundred years before Columbus.

The major problem with the Leif Erikson claim to fame is the scarcity of evidence to support his travels to North America. On the other hand, the expeditions of Columbus had been widely published in Europe. Additionally, the exploits of Columbus inspired others to travel to the "New World" and establish settlements. Therefore, it is not an injustice to Leif Erikson to recognize Columbus as the one who had discovered America.

As to the harsh policies employed by Columbus in his administration of Hispaniola, there is an account that he had two Spaniards sentenced to death for their treatment of certain members of the indigenous population. This contrasts with claims made by detractors of Columbus that he had inflicted pain and suffering upon the native population.

On October 8, 1984, President Ronald Reagan had spoken at a dedication ceremony in Baltimore, Maryland to honor Christopher Columbus. A seventeen-ton statue of Columbus, which had been carved out of marble in Italy, was presented to the city by the Italian-American Organization United and the Italian-American community of Baltimore. In his speech Reagan recognized the contributions to the world made by Columbus and by Italian-Americans to the U.S. Here is an excerpt from his comments:

> *I'm pleased to be here in "Little Italy" with you to honor a man who reminds all Americans that we must always strive for the best, to push to the limits and beyond.*
>
> *Americans of Italian descent have given a great deal to this country. Their contribution began 492 years ago when Christopher Columbus, the son of a Genoa weaver, set forth on a voyage of discovery that changed the world. The ideals which many successive Italian immigrants brought with them are at the very heart of America. I'm speaking of hard work, love of family, patriotism, and respect for God.* [19]

Notwithstanding President Reagan's remarks, a disgruntled group of rioters ripped the statue of Christopher Columbus from its pedestal and dumped it into Baltimore's

---

[19] Ronald Reagan Presidential Library and Museum. (1984, October 8). *Remarks at a Dedication Ceremony for a Statue of Christopher Columbus in Baltimore, Maryland.* Retrieved October 18, 2021, from https://www.reaganlibrary.gov/archives/speech/remarks-dedication-ceremony-statue-christopher-columbus-baltimore-maryland

harbor on July 4, 2020. However, President Donald Trump's administration came to the rescue and awarded thirty thousand dollars in federal funds to recreate the Columbus statue. Sadly, not to be outdone by the anarchists, Baltimore's City Council passed a bill that was signed into law in 2020 to change the name of Columbus Day to Indigenous People's Day.

What is being taught today in our nation's schools about Christopher Columbus? Those "educators" who embrace the nihilists doctrine of cancel culture, portray Columbus in an unflattering manner. Moreover, it is becoming increasingly popular in our public schools to emphasize the plight of the indigenous population in America and placing the blame for it squarely on the shoulders of Columbus. In addition, school boards are under enormous pressure from the federal government to hire teachers from minority backgrounds. Those teachers bring with them their prejudices along with a twisted view of history and of American values. In the classroom, the influence they exercise over impressionable students has provided a pathway for presenting a false narrative of American history and values.

As a case in point, the Clay County School Board in Florida was under pressure by the federal government during the Obama administration to hire teachers of minority backgrounds. Predictably, the school board took a knee and bowed to the demands of the government. Unlike privately funded schools, public schools receive federal funds. The prospect of the loss of funds, gave the county little choice but to accede to the demands of the federal government. The hiring of teachers from minority backgrounds deprived several professionally qualified fulltime and substitute teachers the opportunity to teach in the county.

11. Freemasons and American Values

Freemasons, arguably, are the oldest fraternal order in the U.S. Moreover, our nation was founded upon the principles of Freemasonry. This is without dispute. There is a profound connection between Freemasonry and American values.

At least nine of the fifty-six signers of the Declaration of Independence, including Benjamin Franklin and John Hancock, were known members of a Masonic Lodge.

According to various writers, many of the other signers were alleged to have been in attendance to at least one lodge meeting or had sons who were members of a lodge. Are we going to allow the act of courage it took for each of those signers, who had placed their "John Hancock" (no pun intended) on that document, to be dispatched to the trash bin of history? Will we allow their heroism to be subverted by revisionist history?

Sixteen of our presidents, if you include Thomas Jefferson[20], were Freemasons. Furthermore, the last elected president who was a Freemason was Harry Truman. Additionally, the last sitting president (but unelected) who was a Mason was Gerald Ford. Are we going to allow the cancel culturists to demonize those men through revisionist history by undermining their visionary leadership they had provided to our nation, which enabled it to grow and achieve prosperity?

Monuments and statues have been toppled and vandalized by riotous mobs. Of notable interest to Freemasons, anarchists in Washington, D.C pulled down a statue of General

---

[20] Jefferson's membership in the Craft has been disputed by some writers.

Albert Pike, a Confederate general and Freemason, and set it on fire on June 19, 2020.

According to an article from *Business Insider*, dated June 20, 2020, dozens of people gathered around the statue of General Albert Pike near Judiciary Square, with some chanting "Black Lives Matter" and "Let it Burn."[21] The protesters used ropes and chains to pull down the statue before setting it on fire. President Donald Trump was in disbelief with the inaction of the police who had failed to control the situation. The police did not arrest a single person.

The statue had been erected by an act of Congress, which had approved the acquisition of the land for the memorial in 1898. The Scottish Rite of Freemasonry, of which Pike was a member, had erected the statue in 1901. Then, in 1977, the statue had been placed under the jurisdiction of the National Park Service.

---

[21] Friel, M. (2020, June 20). *Black Lives Matter protesters toppled and burned the capital's only Confederate statue amid Juneteenth celebrations.* Insider. Retrieved December 30, 2021, from https://www.businessinsider.com/black-lives-matter-protesters-burn-washington-dc-confederate-statue-juneteenth-2020-6

The statue portrayed Pike wearing the traditional clothing of a gentleman from the nineteenth century and not in military attire. Additionally, he is shown holding a book he had written about Freemasonry. Notably, the statue did not include any explicit reference to Albert Pike's Confederate service.

This was not the first attempt, however, to remove the statue of Albert Pike. Three years earlier, on or about September 19, 2017, certain members of the D.C. Council introduced a resolution to remove the monument. To the astonishment of the D.C. Council, moving the statue proved to be more difficult than simply passing a council resolution. Since the statue had been erected by an act of congressional approval and had been placed under the jurisdiction of the National Park Service, Congress would have had to pass a bill authorizing its removal. Moreover, the Park Service had to be given oversight of the process.

According to a news story from WAMU.org, dated September 19, 2017, a member of the D.C. Council had said that the Freemasons, whose 16th Street headquarters were in his ward, had supported the removal of the statue. The council member went on to state that the Freemasons had even said

that they would "…provide a flatbed truck to cart the statue out

of the city".[22] Now that is sad!

Notwithstanding the efforts of the D.C. Council to

remove the statue of Albert Pike, the Park Service had rejected

their plan, citing the need for Congress to give its approval

beforehand. Three years later, however, the statue was

unceremoniously destroyed on June 19, 2020, by a group of

dissidents, who thumbed their noses at Congress for its

reluctance to give its approval for the removal of the Pike

memorial.

12. It's Time to Cancel "Cancel Culture"

As the poet, Dylan Thomas, wrote:

"Do not go gentle into that good night,

Old age should burn and rave at close of day;

Rage, rage against the dying of the light."

---

[22] Lefrak, M. (2017, September 19). *D.C. Council Member Says National Park Service Would Charge Him With Trespassing For Removing Confederate Statue.* WAMU 88.5. Retrieved December 30, 2021, from https://wamu.org/story/17/09/19/d-c-council-members-revive-efforts-remove-statue-confederate-backstory/

Will we as a people go gentle into the night? Will we abandon our national heritage, customs, and traditions? Or will we oppose the dying of the light? The light that has been a beacon of hope that our nation has offered to the countless millions of newly arrived legal immigrants over the years.

President John F Kennedy in his inaugural address on January 20, 1961, offered these words:

> *"...Let the word go forth from this time and place to friend and foe alike, that the torch has been passed to a new generation of Americans – born in this century, tempered by war, disciplined by a hard and bitter peace, proud of our ancient heritage..."[23]*

That inaugural address has been referred to as "The Torch is Passed" speech. Those last four words, "...proud of our ancient heritage...", means that we should not allow ourselves to be bullied by others into believing that somehow our nation was born out of racism and grew from oppression. Instead, we should display humbleness in our achievements

---

[23] The Avalon Project. (n.d.) *Inaugural Address of John F. Kennedy.* Yale Law School. Retrieved December 30, 2021, from https://avalon.law.yale.edu/20th_century/kennedy.asp

and confidence in who we are as a people. Moreover, we need to pass along our legacy to a new generation of Americans born in the spirit of hope and optimism.

Let us make manifest our resolve to never surrender our legacy to the forces of "cancel culture". To paraphrase Dylan Thomas, "we will not go quietly into the sunset".

Chapter Eight

Critical Race Theory

1. White Devils

Critical race theory (CRT) is a belief that "systemic racism" and "white supremacy" have been the underlying forces that have led to the development of our nation. Moreover, the advocates of CRT believe that racism continues to persist in our social institutions and is embedded in the laws that govern us as a nation. Incredibly, CRT purports that White people are born in sin, that is, in the sins of slavery, genocide, and the theft of native lands. Its proponents make the unfounded claim that White people, even though they may be poor and culturally disadvantaged, are nevertheless a beneficiary of "racial privilege". In addition, according to the supporters of CRT, federal law has preserved the unequal treatment of people based solely on race. It should come as no surprise then, that the promoters of this narrative have as one of their goals the reframing of the history of the U.S. based on race.

Oprah Winfrey, a television host, engaged in the following exchange with a guest, on her show titled "The Oprah Conversation":

Guest:" Not all White people have power. There's plenty of poor, working-class White people…"

Winfrey: "There are White people who are not as powerful as the system of White people-the caste system that's been put in place. But they still, no matter where they are on the rung or ladder of success, they still have their whiteness." "You still have your whiteness. That's what the term 'White privilege' is. It means that whiteness still gives you an advantage, no matter."[24]

According to Winfrey, if you are White, then you are a privileged person. It doesn't matter if you are a poor, disabled, or culturally challenged White person. Just being born White is a privilege. That coming from a black woman who has an alleged net worth of $2-$3 billion thanks to a predominantly

[24] Sparks, Hannah. (2020, August 5). *Oprah labeled a 'fraud' for calling out 'white privilege' since she's so rich.* New York Post. Retrieved October 19, 2020, from https://nypost.com/2020/08/05/oprah-criticized-for-calling-out-white-privilege-since-shes-rich/

White television audience and White advertisers. It appears Winfrey has been harboring some deep-seated resentment towards White people. What was holding her back all these years? She should have made known her true feelings on race long ago, instead of pretending to befriend her White audience and White advertisers. Someone needs to tell Oprah to let go of her hate and consider herself to be privileged to have had such a successful career.

When the proponents of critical race theory blame systemic racism and White supremacy for the plight of black people, they are making ad hominem attacks on an entire race of people. What they fail to understand, however, is that the White or Caucasian race is made up of many ethnicities. Therefore, when supporters of critical race theory direct their attacks on White people, they are also attacking the ethnicities of Caucasians.

The following European nations are made up of predominantly Caucasian people:

Albania

Andorra

Austria

Belarus

Belgium

Bosnia and Herzegovina

Bulgaria

Croatia

Czech Republic

Denmark

Estonia

Finland

France

Germany

Greece

Hungary

Iceland

Ireland

Italy

Latvia

Liechtenstein

Lithuania

Luxembourg

Malta

Moldova

Monaco

Montenegro

Netherlands

North Macedonia

Norway

Poland

Portugal

Romania

Russia

San Marino

Serbia

Slovakia

Slovenia

Spain

Sweden

Switzerland

Ukraine

United Kingdom

In North America, Canada is a predominantly

Caucasian nation. Mexico, the nations of Central America and

South America are considered Spanish-speaking or Hispanic

nations. Yet many of their inhabitants identify as both Spanish

and White. That is based on responses from Hispanic people

who have immigrated to the U.S. from those lands and have

participated in our nation's census. According to the 2019 U.S.

census, it is estimated that 18.5% of our population is Hispanic.

Moreover, two-thirds of those Hispanics who had responded to

the census identify as White Hispanic. Additionally, the current

census practice is to list White (non-Hispanic) as a race. It is

my understanding that by the middle of the 21st century, there

may be a revision to this practice. White will include those

Hispanics who identify as White Hispanic.

Residents of Puerto Rico speak Spanish but consider

themselves Puerto Rican. As a former colleague told me, "We

are not Spanish. We speak Spanish but are Puerto Rican." If

Puerto Rico became a state, how would those residents identify

racially in the census?

The Caucasian race is one race but many ethnicities. Are all the members comprising those ethnicities to be considered "White supremacists"? When statues of Christopher Columbus are vandalized, who is being assailed by the members of Black Lives Matter and ANTIFA? Is it Christopher Columbus? Or are "White supremacists" and "White colonialists" the object of their wrath? What about the Italian people? Is the ire of Black Lives Matter and ANTIFA directed towards Italian-Americans? What is the response from advocates of critical race theory? How about you Oprah Winfrey? Based on previous remarks by supporters of critical race theory, guilt is to be borne by anybody identifying as a member of the White race. Presumably, that would include members of all ethnicities identified in this section.

2. African Chiefs Enabled the Slave Trade

Slavery had existed in Africa before the White man ventured to the "Dark Continent". African chiefs raided neighboring villages and enslaved their captured enemies. When the British arrived in Africa, those enslaved people were sold to them in return for finished goods. While some Africans were captured and enslaved by English traders, it was African chiefs who had sold their enslaved enemies to the English traders that accounted for the flourishing of the slave trade in Africa. Africans sold Africans for profit.

The name given to the slave trade was the "Triangular Trade". The Triangular Trade was the sailing route across the Atlantic Ocean taken by slave traders. Ships departed England making their way to West Africa. From Africa the ships sailed to the West Indies and colonial North America. A return trip to England from the West Indies and America was the final leg of the journey. Thus, the trade route formed a triangle. Hence the name, the Triangular Trade.

What was being traded among the partners involved in the Triangular Trade? Finished goods, such as, guns, ammunition, cloth, iron products, trinkets, beads, and beer were brought from England to West Africa. They traded those goods for enslaved people, gold, and spices. From Africa, the slave ships which housed the enslaved Africans sailed to the West Indies. In the West Indies, the slaves were sold at auction to plantation owners from colonial North America, along with raw materials, such as sugar and molasses. Once the slave cargo had been sold, the slave ships returned to England carrying sugar, molasses, wood, and other raw materials. From colonial North America, raw materials such as whale oil, lumber, furs, rice, silk, indigo, and tobacco were exported to England. Subsequently, the English used the raw materials to make finished goods. In a ritualistic manner, the process repeated itself, over and over again.

3. Critical Race Theory Invades the Military

Like a virus spreading throughout the nation, our military is not immune to the malignancy of critical race theory. Congressman Michael Waltz (R-FL) had written a letter in 2021 to Lieutenant General Darryl Williams, Superintendent at West Point, regarding information that had come to his attention from concerned soldiers, cadets, and their families about the introduction of critical race theory into cadet instruction. Waltz is also a U.S. Army officer. He had emphatically detailed his concerns that instruction in critical race theory focused on race in ways that could be detrimental to unit cohesiveness and lead to a destruction in morale.[25]

Waltz, appearing on Fox News in an interview with Tucker Carlson, stated he had received notice of a West Point lecture titled, "Understanding Whiteness and White Rage". He added that some families with whom he had spoken were concerned about its content.[26]

Who is Lieutenant General Darryl Williams, Superintendent at West Point? He is a career Army officer. He is black. He is the 60th superintendent at West Point.

Notably, he is the first black superintendent at West Point in its 216-year history. For the sake of this nation, I pray that he will not advance any radical agenda on race at West Point. It would be a black eye (no pun intended) to the historic history of the academy and to its cadets.

---

[25] Phillips, J. (2021, April 11). *'Critical Race Theory' Being Taught at US Army's West Point: Congressman*. NTD. Retrieved January 3, 2022, from https://www.ntd.com/critical-race-theory-being-taught-at-us-armys-west-point-congressman_595616.html
[26] Ibid.

4. Radicals at the Federal Reserve Banks

The mission of the Federal Reserve is to achieve

maximum employment along with stable prices. The Fed is to

follow those objectives while maintaining its independence

from any political influence. In other words, the Federal

Reserve is to operate as an independent central bank.

Politicization of the Fed jeopardizes its ability to operate freely

in the best interests of our nation.

Federal Reserve banks in Atlanta, Boston, and

Minneapolis, however, have violated their mandate of

independence from political influence by becoming "woke".

Senator Pat Toomey (R-PA), the ranking member of the Senate

Banking Committee, has sounded the alarm by admonishing

those banks for having taken a stance on highly charged issues

such as racial justice.[27]

Those three banks had called a meeting attended by all

twelve regional banks to promote a series titled, "Racism and

---

[27] Garber, J. (2021, May 27). *Wokeness at Fed's regional banks puts central bank independence at risk.* Fox Business. Retrieved May 27, 2021, from https://www.foxbusiness.com/economy/wokeness-fed-regional-banks-independence-at-risk

Economy". The underlying tenet of the series was based on the belief that "racism forms the foundation of inequality in our society." Among the topics to be discussed was structural racism in housing, education, and labor markets.[28]

Moreover, the Atlanta Fed president, Raphael Bostic, the first black Fed president, has stated that if he were to become chairman of the Fed, he would push the central bank toward economic inclusivity and equity. He added that there were "definitely merits" to reparations for blacks. In addition, he had also published a letter titled, "A Moral and Economic Imperative to End Racism."[29]

Furthermore, the Minneapolis Fed in its 2020 annual report pledged its unswerving commitment to the dismantling of systemic racism. Not to be outdone by its Minneapolis counterpart, the Boston Fed published a report stating that the deaths of George Floyd and others were the result of the "racist roots of this country".[30] Of course, no mention was made of the

---

[28] Ibid.
[29] Ibid.
[30] Ibid.

criminal lifestyle and numerous convictions of the black felon, George Floyd. Just blame it on society!

How serious is this politicization of the Fed? Before we answer that question, let us review the history of the concept of a central banking system in the U.S.

Several of the Founding Fathers were suspicious of a national banking system. The major reason for their opposition to a central bank was that England had tried to place the colonies under the monetary control of the Bank of England. Thomas Jefferson fiercely opposed the concept of a central bank. In addition, he strongly distrusted banks and bankers. He's not alone.

On the other hand, Alexander Hamilton advocated for a national banking system. Notwithstanding George Washington's distrust of a central bank, he was persuaded by Alexander Hamilton in 1791 to approve a charter for the First Bank of the U.S. In addition, Washington appointed Hamilton as the first secretary of the U.S. treasury. Hamilton you may recall is best remembered in history because of a duel he had with the vice-president of the U.S., Aaron Burr. The duel took place on July 11, 1804. Hamilton was fatally wounded on that day

The charter for the First Bank of the U.S. was for a term of twenty years. At the end of its 20-year term, the charter was not renewed, and the bank became defunct in 1811.

The charter for a Second Bank of the U.S. was for a similar 20-year term from 1816-1836. President Andrew Jackson, however, went to war with the banking system and denounced the bank as an "engine of corruption". Although Jackson could not rescind the charter, he nevertheless destroyed the bank by refusing to renew its charter.

Advocates for "big banks" despised "Old Hickory", Jackson's nickname earned in battle during the War of 1812 and in fighting Indians. They never forgave him for destroying the Second Bank of the U.S. That hate has been passed on down through the generations and extends to this day.

When plans were made to replace Alexander Hamilton's portrait on the $10 bill with that of a female abolitionist, it was suggested that it would be more fitting to replace Andrew Jackson's likeness on the $20 bill rather than that of Alexander Hamilton. The reasoning was that Hamilton was a supporter of a national banking system, unlike Jackson who despised large banks. As of the date of this writing, changes to the $20 bill were scheduled to take place in the near term.

There is an old saying, "Be careful what you wish for, you just may get it." Well, we got it, in the form of a central banking system, courtesy of the U.S. Congress and President Woodrow Wilson. It is the Federal Reserve System. The Fed was created in 1913 by the Federal Reserve Act. For good or for worse, it has become a permanent institution in our financial system.

Based upon our review of the history of banking in the U.S., especially given the strong opposition to a central bank by the early leaders of our nation, any politicization of the Fed is arguably a bad idea. Since its inception, however, the power of the Fed has continued to grow in an alarming manner. The power granted to it by the Federal Reserve Act, allows the Fed to operate outside the reach of Congress and the president. Unchecked and unregulated, it can ignore the economic wishes of both those branches of government. It has become a "shadow government". That does not bode well for our economic wellbeing.

Can you imagine the harm somebody such as Atlanta Fed President, Raphael Bostic, the first black Fed president, could inflict on this nation's economy, if he were to become chairman of the Fed? As stated earlier, he has gone on record calling for reparations for black members of society. What could reparations for black people look like in practice? One recommendation being considered is to grant black people zero-interest mortgages or to have the government forgive their mortgage debt. Its aim would be to place more blacks on the path to home ownership. In addition, the plan would allow black families to move into neighborhoods that hitherto were predominantly White. According to its proponents, this would reduce racial inequality in society and structural racism in housing.

Reparations for blacks, as an economic policy, is patently racist. Moreover, providing reparations to the black community would irreparably strain the social fabric of our nation. We cannot allow this to happen to our nation. There must be a day of reckoning for the Fed. It cannot continue to operate in an unrestrained manner. The sooner it is held accountable for its actions, the better it will be for our nation.

5. Debt Forgiveness for Black Farmers and Ranchers

The U.S. government by way of the Department of Agriculture was prepared to provide debt relief payments to thousands of "socially disadvantaged farmers and ranchers" beginning in June 2021.[31] There is one catch. Only black farmers and ranchers qualify as recipients. The program patently discriminated against White farmers and ranchers, however, regardless of their economic or social standing.

Not surprisingly, there have been multiple lawsuits brought by White farmers alleging discrimination against American farmers based solely on their race. One of the lawsuits has resulted in a federal judge in Wisconsin issuing a

---

[31] Henney, M. (2021, May 24). USDA to start debt forgiveness for Black farmers in June. Fox Business. Retrieved May 24, 2021, from https://www.foxbusiness.com/economy/usda-debt-forgiveness-black-farmers-june

nationwide temporary injunction to halt the implementation of the program. Moreover, there is a high probability that the U.S. Supreme Court may eventually hear the case and render a final decision. It appears our nation has come a long way since "40 acres and a mule".

6. "40 Acres and a Mule" in the 21ˢᵗ Century

What was "40 acres and a mule"? In U.S. history, we were told that the slogan referred to the government's program to reward former slaves with land from Southern states confiscated during the Civil War. Did the former slaves actually receive the land and mules? Initially, the former slaves did receive land formerly held by Southern planters. Their land ownership, however, was of short duration. Let's examine what really happened to "40 acres and a mule".

Towards the conclusion of the War Between the States, General William T. Sherman issued a field order in January 1865, which called for 40 acres of land to be distributed to recently freed slaves. In total, "Sherman's Land", comprised approximately 400,000 acres along the South Carolina,

Georgia, and Florida coasts. By June 1865, 40,000 former

slaves or freedmen had settled on the land. However, they had

no farm animals with which to work the land. Sherman then

ordered that the new occupants of the land would be provided

with mules, courtesy of the U.S. Army. Following the

assassination of Abraham Lincoln, Andrew Johnson became

president of the U.S. Johnson, however, did not approve of

Sherman's order and overturned it in the fall of 1865. The

lands that were given to the freedmen were returned to their

original owners.

In the context of "racial equality", "40 acres and a

mule" may be viewed as the first attempt by the U.S.

government to provide reparations to black Americans. Land

redistribution has been a concept that has been discussed since

the end of the Civil War.

On November 19, 2020, U.S. Senators Cory Booker (D-

NJ), Elizabeth Warren (D-MA), Kirsten Gillibrand (D-NY),

Tina Smith (D-MN), Raphael Warnock (D-GA), and Patrick

Leahy (D-VT) announced legislation that would redistribute

farmland to existing and future black farmers. The bill, "Justice for Black Farmers Act", would create an "Equitable Land Access Service" within the U.S. Department of Agriculture (USDA). Its prime directive would be to acquire farmland and provide land grants of up to 160 acres to black farmers. Both current and future black farmers would be the recipients of this "landfall". Additionally, black farmers would be able to access USDA loans and mortgages on very generous terms.[32] From "40 acres and a mule" to "160 acres and free money" is quite an improvement.

Sadly, this attempt at land redistribution is nothing more than an endeavor to implement Socialist ideology, whereby, land is taken from the "haves" and given to the "have-nots" under the guise of racial equity. As improbable as it may seem, we are nearing the time when such land reform may become a reality.

---

[32] Senator Cory Booker. (2021, February 9). *Booker, Warren, Gillibrand, Smith, Warnock, and Leahy Announce Comprehensive Bill to Address the History of Discrimination in Federal Agricultural Policy.* Retrieved January 3, 2022, from *https://www.booker.senate.gov/news/press/booker-warren-gillibrand-smith-warnock-and-leahy-announce-comprehensive-bill-to-address-the-history-of-discrimination-in-federal-agricultural-policy*

There is an interesting parallel that can be made between the U.S. and South Africa. Both nations have witnessed attempts at land reform to achieve racial equality. One enormous difference between South Africa and the U.S., however, is their racial demographics. In South Africa, blacks were estimated to comprise 81% of the population, based on 2017 estimates.[33] On the other hand, Whites were estimated to represent 8% of the population.[34] In the U.S., however, our racial demographics reveal a predominantly White population. According to estimates from the 2019 U.S. Census Bureau, the White race (including those of Hispanic descent who identify as White) represented approximately 73% of our population. Blacks, on the other hand, comprised just over 13% of the population. That is quite a contrast between South Africa and the U.S. In South Africa, blacks are the predominant race, whereas, in the U.S. the predominant race is White.

---

[33] Alexander, MC. (2018, July 9). *South Africa's population.* South Africa Gateway. Retrieved January 3, 2022, from https://southafrica-info.com/people/south-africa-population/
[34] Ibid.

South Africa was once an apartheid nation. The black population is not only the predominant race in South Africa, however, it is also the dominant force in the South African government. Once apartheid had ended, the government began a program of land redistribution. It consisted of seizing land from White landowners but providing compensation to them for the seized land. A proposed law would change that to the detriment of White landowners. The law would specify the conditions under which land may be confiscated (expropriated) without compensation.[35] Courts would have the final say on the amount of compensation and each grievance would be adjudicated on a case-by-case basis. The ruling African National Congress (ANC), however, has stated it intends to speed up the process by amending the Constitution to allow for the expropriation of land without compensation.[36] It was still being debated as of June 2, 2021.

---

[35] Reuters Staff. (2020, October 11). *South Africa lays out conditions to seize land, says investors will be reassured.* Reuters. Retrieved January 3, 2022, from https://www.reuters.com/article/safrica-land/south-africa-lays-out-conditions-to-seize-land-says-investors-will-be-reassured-idUSKBN26W0RS
[36] Ibid.

The U.S., on the other hand, was never an apartheid nation. It is true that slavery existed in the colonies and in the early years of the Republic. A great war, however, engulfed our nation and decided the issue of slavery. The end of slavery was paid for with the blood of both Union and Confederate forces. We emerged from that war bloodied but a united people. Although "40 acres and a mule" was short-lived, there have been a litany of reparations given to the black community over the ensuing years. Subsidized housing, food stamps, free medical care, welfare payments, and preferential treatment in job placement are just some of the reparations that have been handed to the black community. However, the demands by Senators Booker, Warren, Gillibrand, and others to redistribute farmland to existing and future black farmers is a bit of a stretch. In addition, so is their proposal to provide black farmers with free money to maintain and work the farms.

Furthermore, the program of debt forgiveness for black farmers and ranchers to the exclusion of their White counterparts by the Department of Agriculture is a mockery of equal treatment under the law. I dare say that if the black population were the predominant race in the U.S. and also the dominant force in our government, there would be a movement to confiscate the land of White owners without compensation, similar to what is taking place in South Africa. The ruling powers would justify the theft of land under the guise of "racial equity". Therefore, we must be vigilant to the threat of socialist propaganda that advocates for a redistribution of land under the pretense of racial justice and racial equity. If we do not, then woe to our children and grandchildren. Under such circumstances, they would be the ones who would bear the indignity and pain brought upon them by our lack of vigilance.

7. Department of Defense vs. State Department

U.S. embassies were authorized to fly Black Lives Matter (BLM) flags to commemorate the one-year anniversary of the death of George Floyd, a black felon. Floyd died on May 25, 2020, in an altercation with police in Minneapolis. A memo released by the State Department encouraged embassies as well as consulates to consider the need to eliminate systemic racism and fly the BLM flag. The Department of Defense (DOD), however, did not share the State Department's sentiment. Therefore, no BLM flags were flown on military installations.

Furthermore, the Defense Department refused to fly the "Pride" flag at military installations to commemorate LGBTQ (Lesbian, Gay, Bisexual, Transgender, and Queer) Pride month. Pride month is currently observed each year in the month of June. On the other hand, the State Department took an opposite stance from the DOD on flying the Pride flag. In a reversal of the Trump administration's policy that banned the flying of the Pride flag at embassies, the State Department stated that it would allow the Pride flag to be displayed at U.S. diplomatic outposts and embassies. While diplomatic posts were given the option to fly the Pride flag, the State Department advised that caution should nevertheless be exercised to determine that such displays were appropriate in foreign lands.

It should be remembered that homosexuality and lesbianism are not culturally accepted in many of the nations of the world. In general, Islamic scholars teach that to engage in gender sex is a sin. In Middle Eastern and North African countries homosexuality has been criminalized with sentences that range from prison terms to the death penalty. Therefore, it would behoove our embassy leaders to consider a nation's culture and its moral code regarding the gay lifestyle before a Pride flag is flown at those installations. They need to remember the old adage, "When in Rome, do as the Romans do". In this case, do not offend the local population by insisting on flying the Pride flag in a display of arrogance.

8. Special Instructions for White People

At the George Floyd Square in Minneapolis stands a memorial to the convicted felon. It features special instructions for White people. A sign near the entrance of the square welcomes its visitors to "A Sacred Place for Community, Public Grief, and Protest". Visitors are urged to "Enter with reverence, humility, and openness, as an invited guest". Moreover, it states that, "For White people in particular: Decenter yourself and come to listen, learn, mourn, and witness. Remember you are here to support, not to be supported."[37]

Since the death of George Floyd, the area has been converted into an "autonomous zone". The "zone", however, has ushered in record setting levels of violent crime and gun violence. Moreover, armed individuals (thugs) have rolled out the unwelcome mat for law enforcement. Additionally, local businesses have had their operations disrupted by gang activity, drug dealers, and gun violence. Truly, a testament to George Floyd.

9. Juneteenth or "Jubilee Day"

June 19 officially became a federal holiday in the U.S. in June 2021. The newest federal holiday is to commemorate the emancipation of black slaves in the U.S. The holiday is called Juneteenth, the blending of June and nineteenth. The proponents of critical race theory consider it to be the day in

---

[37] Betz, B. (2021, April 21). *Minneapolis' George Floyd Square features special instructions for White people.* Fox News. Retrieved April 21, 2021, from https://www.foxnews.com/us/minneapolis-george-floyd-square-special-instructions-white-people

1865 when black slaves had received their freedom or independence. It is their independence day.

The Emancipation Proclamation, issued by President Abraham Lincoln, however, is widely considered to have freed the slaves in the U.S. Lincoln had issued an executive order on September 22, 1862 that took effect on January 1, 1863, freeing the slaves in Confederate states that were in rebellion against the Union. The War Between the States finally ended on April 9, 1865, when General Robert E. Lee, Commanding General of the Confederate forces, surrendered to General Ulysses S. Grant, Commanding General of the Union Army at Appomattox Courthouse in Virginia. Nothing is official, however, until somebody declares it official. That someone was President Andrew Johnson who declared a formal end to the conflict in August 1866.

Although the de facto end of the war had occurred with Lee's surrender to Grant, there were slaves in Texas who were kept in the dark (no pun intended) about the cessation of hostilities and their ensuing freedom. With the arrival of federal troops in Galveston, Texas in June 1865, slaves were given the good news that the chains that had shackled them were going to be removed forever.

The cry went out to all slaves in Texas, "We are free! Time to celebrate jubilee!" Thereafter, commencing with June 19,1866, "Jubilee Day" has been celebrated annually commemorating the emancipation of black slaves in the U.S.

Although the slaves in the Confederate states may have gained their freedom, it would require the ratification of the 13th Amendment to the Constitution in December 1865 to abolish slavery in the United States. Was slavery really abolished with the passage of the 13th Amendment? What is the text of the 13th Amendment? It reads as follows:

Section 1. Neither slavery nor involuntary servitude, *except as a punishment for crime whereof the party shall have been duly convicted*, shall exist within the United States, or any place subject to their jurisdiction.

Section 2. Congress shall have power to enforce this article by appropriate legislation.[38]

[38] National Constitution Center. (n.d.). *13th Amendment*. Retrieved January 3, 2022, from https://constitutioncenter.org/interactive-constitution/amendment/amendment-xiii

There is an exception for slavery and involuntary servitude. Both slavery and involuntary servitude were abolished, "except as a punishment for crime whereof the party shall have been duly convicted". That loophole to the 13th Amendment has never been closed to this day. In 2020, however, members of Congress had addressed the issue and had proposed a resolution which would close the loophole to the 13th Amendment. However, it would need to pass both houses of Congress by a two-thirds majority and would need to be approved by three-quarters of the states.

Is there a problem with amending the 13th Amendment? The answer is, yes. Amending our Constitution because of pressure from minority groups, radical news media outlets, and various socialist organizations weakens its integrity. For example, what if some group wants to rewrite the Second Amendment to disallow private citizens the right to bear arms, under the pretext that abolishing guns in the hands of private citizens would save lives? Should Congress yield to their demand?

The elevation of Juneteenth to the status of a federal holiday conflicts with Independence Day which is celebrated on the 4th of July. There cannot be two independence days; nor can there be two national anthems. We now have June 19 and July 4 as established federal holidays of independence. There are also "The Star-Spangled Banner" and a black national anthem. A nation can have only one Independence Day and one national anthem. Try and tell that to the radical elements who are spreading hate and trying to split us apart along racial lines.

There are some very vociferous elements of society that have been clamoring to replace July 4th with June 19th. A former professional football player had the audacity to denounce the 4th of July as a "celebration of white supremacy." Moreover, members of various radical groups are in complete support of that contention. They present a tendentious reading of our nation's events and wish to rewrite its history.

Notwithstanding the objections of those who denigrate our nation's institutions, culture, history, and holidays, July 4th may prove difficult for them to erase from our calendar. One reason is that July 4th is a federal holiday. Translation, a paid federal holiday for many people. Not many persons, including black people, would want to surrender a paid federal holiday for a radical idea. Another reason is that many families plan their summer vacation during the first week of July. Would they prefer moving it up two weeks to the week encompassing June 19th? Somehow July feels more like summer than does June.

10. Destruction of America's Pastime

Like a cancer that begins to form in a localized region of the human body and then spreads as a horde of locusts throughout every internal organ, critical race theory has also wreaked havoc on America's favorite pastime - sports. From taking a knee as a form of protest of the American flag and the National Anthem, to advocating for support of Black Lives Matter, America's athletes have turned off its fanbase, dealing a severe blow to the public's enjoyment of sports.

In June 2021, one of the black basketball analysts at

ESPN (the CNN of sports), stated that he was disappointed that

a White professional basketball player, Kevin Love, had been

added to the Olympic basketball roster of team USA.

Moreover, he railed that the reason Love had been selected to

be on the squad was because of "tokenism".[39] That is, it was

because Love was White, and the selection committee wanted

at least one White player on the team. Additionally, the analyst

added that he was equally disappointed that an all-black

basketball team was not representing the U.S. at the

Olympics.[40] He continued his disparagement of Love by

alleging that Love did not deserve to be on the squad because

he was not the best available player.[41] If we reverse the racial

roles and it had been a White basketball analyst who had made

those disparaging remarks calling for an all-White basketball

---

[39] Gaydos, R. (2021, June 24). *Kevin Love made US Olympic team because of 'tokenism', ESPN's Jalen Rose says.* Fox News. Retrieved June 24, 2021, from https://www.foxnews.com/sports/kevin-love-us-olympic-team-tokenism-espn-jalen-rose
[40] Ibid.
[41] Ibid.

team at the Olympics, is there any doubt that person would have been relieved of his duties?

A few days after the analyst at ESPN ran his racist mouth off about being disappointed that an all-black basketball team was not representing the U.S. at the Olympics, another incident occurred at the women's U.S. Olympic Track and Field Trials in Eugene, Oregon. During the playing of the National Anthem at the medal ceremony for the women's hammer throw, the third-place finisher, a black female, was seen pouting, turning her back on the flag, and pulling her shirt over her head. A totally disrespectful display by an American Olympic athlete towards our flag and anthem.

On the other hand, the top two finishers, both White women, were standing at attention facing the flag with their hands held over their hearts. The black female athlete rambled that the anthem did not speak for her and never had, but that she was there to represent those persons who had died because of systemic racism.[42] Did that female belong in the Olympics as a representative of the U.S.?

The Summer Olympics, officially the Games of the XXXII Olympiad, were scheduled to be held from July 23 through August 8, 2021, in Tokyo, Japan. Will black American athletes stage any protests and perform any demonstrations at this international event? It is my hope that all American athletes will conduct themselves in the utmost professional manner and with dignity.

11. From Little Black Sambo to Black Lives Matter

In this chapter, we have examined the precepts of critical race theory. In addition, we noted its effect on the Army, Department of Defense and State Department. Moreover, we discussed the program at the Department of Agriculture that would provide debt forgiveness to black

---

[42] Dedaj, P. (2021, June 27). *Gwen Berry turns back to US flag during national anthem at Olympic trials, says she was 'set-up'.* Fox News. Retrieved June 27, 2021, from https://www.foxnews.com/sports/message-sent-berry-turns-away-from-flag-during-anthem

farmers and ranchers. Furthermore, we commented on the Federal Reserve's desire to promote economic racial equity. Other events we had discussed were the construction of a memorial to the notorious felon, George Floyd; the passage of legislation creating another Federal holiday, Juneteenth; and the ruination of American sports. In all those instances, critical race theory played a significant role.

The rest of this section will explore the effect that critical race theory has had on education. When I had attended first grade, my favorite reader was *The Story of Little Black Sambo*. To this day, I can still visualize those three tigers chasing each other around a tree and turning themselves into butter. Little Black Sambo then collects the butter in a bucket and brings it home to his mother, Black Mumbo, so that they can enjoy warm butter over their pancakes. That book had been the favorite of first grade students in the U.S. from the beginning of the 20th century up until the early 1960s. It was read by future presidents, military leaders, scientists, members of the clergy, entertainers, lawyers, doctors, teachers, nurses, used car salesmen, professional athletes, farmers, industrial workers, garbage collectors, and anybody who had attended public school during those years. Additionally, many fine school children were influenced by the writings of Helen Bannerman (*The Story of Little Black Sambo*), Mark Twain (*The Adventures of Tom Sawyer*), William Shakespeare (*Romeo and Juliet, Macbeth, Hamlet*) and other authors. The written works of those writers were profoundly embraced by generations of Americans, including the World War II generation, nicknamed "The Greatest Generation". That is the generation who had successfully fought the Fascists in Europe and the Imperial Japanese Empire in the Pacific during World War II. They brought justice and peace to a world decimated by the policies of dictatorial regimes.

Unfortunately, those writers and their works have been the object of scorn by the advocates of critical race theory. Those who decry American greatness contend that the works of those writers inspired generations of racists and promoted systemic racism. Moreover, they sternly condemn generations of Americans, including "The Greatest Generation", as racists and the beneficiaries of racial privilege. Nothing could be further from the truth!

The supporters of critical race theory had banned *The Story of Little Black Sambo* decades ago from our nation's public schools. In having done so, they have deprived countless number of school children the pleasure of reading a classic story that would have piqued their interest and would have had a positive influence on their development into adulthood. More recently, the works of Mark Twain (Samuel Clemens), William Shakespeare, and even Dr. Seuss (Theodor Seuss Geisel) have become the objects of scorn by the radical supporters of critical race theory. The iconoclasts seek to have those cherished works banned in schools on the pretext that the writings reinforce and promote systemic racism. Instead, the proponents of critical race theory would replace those works with writings that teach children about Black Lives Matter and cancel culture. Let us hopscotch around our nation and look at some of the damage being done to our school children in the name of critical race theory.

On the East Coast in East Providence, RI is the Gordon School. It is a coeducational, independent school that is open to children from nursery through eighth grade. Parents at the school founded a group called the "Antiracism Working Group for White Parents". The group provides "opportunities for White parents to examine their own racial identities and privilege, to uncover and challenge their own biases, and to develop anti-racism parenting skills." A series of "parent dialogues" had been scheduled for the 2020-2021 academic year. One of the readings was titled, "The Characteristics of White Supremacy Culture." Would you want your child enrolled in that school? (Many of the Gordon School's web pages were inaccessible at the time of the proofing of this manuscript. No explanation was given on their home page, https://www.gordonschool.org/apply-home/discover, which was retrieved on January 4, 2022.)

Travelling northward by auto on Rhode Island's pot-holed roads will lead you into Massachusetts. Our destination is Brandeis University, a private institution of higher learning in Waltham, Massachusetts.

At the time of this writing, there was an assistant dean at the school by the name of Kate Slater. Her website described her as "a White anti-racist scholar and educator" who believes "that a core pillar of racial social justice work is the redistribution of resources to people of color". [43] She has been cited as having stated that "all White people are racist" and that she hated "Whiteness".[44] That is a lot of hate coming from a young woman. Moreover, she has defended teaching critical race theory in the classroom. Would you want her teaching critical race theory propaganda to your child?

In Virginia's Loudoun County, critical race theory has been a polarizing and controversial issue that has driven a wedge in the community. It has pitted neighbor against neighbor and teacher against teacher. A large number of both parents and teachers have strongly opposed the county's plans to pressure teachers into complying with the unpopular

---

[43] Kate Slater. Retrieved January 4, 2022, from https://kateaslater.com/about
[44] Lungariello, M. (2021, May 26). *White Brandeis Dean Kate Slater posts epic critical race theory rant: 'I hate whiteness'.* New York Post. Retrieved May 26, 2021, from https://nypost.com/2021/05/26/white-brandeis-dean-kate-slater-posts-critical-race-theory-rant/

mandate to "disrupt and dismantle this systemic racism".[45] Not surprisingly, the county has vigorously denied that it is promoting critical race theory. Notwithstanding such denial, the school district has accused Dr. Seuss books of promoting "racial undertones".[46] Dr. Seuss a racist?

Things have gotten entirely out of hand, however, in the county. A group that has become known as the "Anti-Racist Parents of Loudoun County" have allegedly compiled a list of those persons who have opposed the teaching of critical race theory.[47] In addition, the members of the group have purportedly attempted to track and "dox" their opponents.[48] Comments by alleged group members have led to the listing of the names, addresses, and places of employment of members of the community with whom they have had disagreements. [49]

---

[45] Dorman, S. (2021, April 16). *Virginia teacher says critical race theory has damaged community as frustrated parents demand changes.* Fox News. Retrieved April 16, 2021, from https://www.foxnews.com/us/loudoun-county-critical-race-theory-divided
[46] Ibid.
[47] Ibid.
[48] Ibid.
[49] Ibid.

The situation in Loudoun County has not only strained the relationships among members in the community but has had a disruptive influence in the classroom. The promotion of propaganda is an unpopular idea among parents and teachers. Would you want a radical agenda forced upon your children?

The Big Apple has its proponents of critical race theory. One such person, a principal at the East Side Community School in New York, had a dream. His dream was to convert "White supremacists" into "White abolitionists". A list was sent to White parents by the principal titled, "The 8 White Identities".[50] Its purpose was to urge White parents to convert themselves from "White supremacists" to "White abolitionists".[51]

The eight white identities ranged from:

1. White supremacist

2. White voyeurism

---

[50] Hoft, J. (2021, February 16). *Pure Racism: New York City Principal Sends Home White Identities List to Parents to Covert Them to the "White Traitors" Stage of Whiteness.* Gateway Pundit. Retrieved February 16, 2021, from https://www.thegatewaypundit.com/2021/02/pure-racism-new-york-city-principal-sends-home-white-identities-list-parents-convert-white-traitors-stage-whiteness/?utm_source=Email&utm_medium=the-gateway-pundit&utm_campaign=dailyam&utm_content=daily
[51] Ibid.

3. White privilege

4. White benefit

5. White confessional

6. White critical

7. White traitor

8. White abolitionist[52]

According to the directive, people who identify with "Whiteness" fall into one of those eight categories. The objective is to ultimately make the journey to the "White abolitionist" stage which is described as, "Changing institutions, dismantling whiteness, and not allowing whiteness to reassert itself." [53]

It is appalling that someone with that kind of thought process was hired to lead an educational institution. Do you think he should have his contract rescinded and be removed from his administrative post?

On the West Coast (or "left coast") students at a middle school in Orange County, CA were asked to analyze an op-ed

---

[52] Ibid.
[53] Ibid.

that had been published five years earlier in 2016 in the

Huffington Post titled, "Why I'm a Racist".[54] According to

several parents, their children felt uncomfortable with the

assignment. Who would not feel uncomfortable with that

assignment?

Moreover, the State of California was close to

implementing a statewide curriculum titled, "Ethnic Studies

Model Curriculum" which had been approved by lawmakers in

2021.[55] It urged high schools to introduce students to stories of

so-called marginalized peoples that are usually not found in

U.S. history courses. Although the new curriculum was not a

mandatory requirement, a bill had been introduced in the

California General Assembly that would require high school

students to complete one full year of ethnic studies as a

prerequisite to graduation beginning with the 2025-2026 school

year.[56] Thus, high school graduates would have to complete

---

[54] Conklin, A. (2021, June 3). *California middle schoolers get 'uncomfortable' assignment of Huffington Post op-ed, 'Why I'm a Racist'.* Fox News. Retrieved June 3, 2021, from https://www.foxnews.com/us/california-middle-schoolers-huffington-post-op-ed
[55] Ibid.
[56] Ibid.

two semesters (a full year) of ethnic studies to receive their diplomas. As Confucius would have said, "No tickee, no payee!" Is it any wonder that so many Californians are fleeing their state?

Furthermore, California and its neighbor to the north, Oregon, have suggested that math must be dismantled because it contains racist elements. The Department of Education in Oregon has encouraged teachers to register for training that promotes "ethnomathematics".[57] Moreover, it has issued a toolkit titled, "Equitable Math",[58] as a guide to dismantling racism in mathematics. Furthermore, part of the toolkit includes a list of ways that White supremacy manifests itself in math. It does so, according to the guide, by focusing on finding the "right answer" and requiring students "to show their work". Additionally, teachers are advised to provide at least two answers that might solve a problem. They are also instructed to

---

[57] Dorman, S. (2021, February 12). *Oregon promotes teacher program that seeks to undo 'racism in mathematics'.* Fox News. Retrieved February 12, 2021, from https://www.foxnews.com/us/oregon-education-math-white-supremacy
[58] Ibid.

identify and challenge the ways in which math is utilized to support capitalist, imperialist, and racist viewpoints.

That is truly an amazing position that has been taken by the Oregon Department of Education. Declaring war on math without any evidence to support their outrageous contentions defies all logic.

Math has been declared the "universal language" by mathematicians, physicists, scientists, and scholars since it was developed by man for his use in the betterment of humanity. No matter what language we speak, from English to Mandarin, math is the one language we all have in common. Math has helped us build things, save money, manage time, discover new cures for disease, send a man to the moon, communicate to others by cellphone, and in countless other ways. It was used by the Egyptians to build their pyramids, helped the Three Wise Men locate the star of Bethlehem that indicated the birthplace of Jesus, and enabled the Chinese to build their Great Wall. Every one of those groups of people spoke a different language but shared the one language they could all understand, math.

If the Departments of Education in Oregon and in other states intend to weaken math, have they given any thought as to what they intend to use as a replacement? Or do they intend to return us to the Stone Age?

Our next stop is in the heartland and the great state of Missouri. Middle school teachers in Springfield attended a diversity training session on race. At the seminar, the teachers were told that "White supremacy" included ideas such as "all lives matter", "claiming reverse-racism", "calling the police on black people", and "colorblindness".[59] Since when did a belief in "all lives matter" make someone a "White supremacist"? They call this "diversity training"? "Perversity training" would be a more appropriate term.

There is a public elementary school in the Denver, Colorado area that is planning to indoctrinate kindergarten and first-grade students on gender and race sensitivity as part of an effort to teach the principles of the Black Lives Matter

---

[59] Dorman, S. (2021, January 21). *Missouri diversity session tells teachers 'color blindness', 'all lives matter' are forms of white supremacy.* Fox News. Retrieved January 21, 2021, from https://www.foxnews.com/politics/missouri-diversity-training-teachers-white-supremacy

movement.[60] According to the website of, Centennial-A School

of Expeditionary Learning:

> "Our students all engaged in a two-week learning
>
> and discussion series around the 13 principles of the
>
> BLM@School Organization."[61]

Yikes!

Miguel Cardona was the U.S. secretary of education in

2021. He was the former commissioner of education for the

state of Connecticut. As the top educational leader in

Connecticut, Cardona's department was instrumental in the

creation of a new high school course centered around African

American, Black, Puerto Rican, and Latino Studies.[62] The state

approved the curriculum in December 2020.[63] In so doing, it

---

[60] Miller, A.M. (2022, January 21). *Denver public school teaching kindergartners BLM 'guiding principles' including 'disruption of nuclear family'.* Fox News. Retrieved March 4, 2022, from https://www.foxnews.com/politics/denver-public-school-teaching-kindergartners-blm-guiding-principles-including-disruption-nuclear-family

[61] Centennial, A School for Expeditionary Learning. (n.d.). *Equity Work-Students: BLM@School Week of Action.* Retrieved March 4, 2022, from https://centennial.dpsk12.org/equity/equity-work-students/

[62] Olson, T. (2021, April 27). *Education Secretary Miquel Cardona worried about getting teachers behind new 'woke' curriculum in email.* Fox News. Retrieved April 27, 2021, from https://www.foxnews.com/politics/education-secretary-miguel-cardona-worried-about-getting-teachers-behind-woke-curriculum

[63] Ibid.

made Connecticut the first state in the nation to require all high schools to offer the course. The curriculum would be optional until the school year beginning in the fall of 2022, when it would become mandatory.

The Connecticut curriculum would implore students to understand the construct of race including the how and why of its development. In addition, it mandates that there must be ample time dedicated to "systemic racism" and the Black Lives Matter movement. Moreover, other topics to be addressed include a discussion of slavery, what "African American, Black, Latino, and Puerto Rican histories reveal about the United States", the nation's foundation, and how power is structured today in our nation.

Furthermore, there was concern that Cardona intended to advocate for a nationwide curriculum that would be "woke" (become alert to injustices in society, especially racism). If that became a nationwide educational requirement, it would mark the tipping point in the fight for the survival of our nation's public schools. Do we want this radical agenda to become the law of the land?

12. Opposition to Critical Race Theory

Oklahoma fights back. The Governor of Oklahoma signed into law in 2021 a new bill that stated, "no teacher shall require or make part of a course that one race or sex is inherently superior to another race or sex". In addition, the law banned the teaching of concepts such as "an individual by virtue of his or her race or sex bears responsibility for actions committed in the past by other members of the same race or sex". Moreover, the law prevents teaching students that "any individual should feel discomfort, guilt, anguish, or any other form or psychological disgrace on account of his or her race or sex". Furthermore, educators are prohibited from teaching that principles such as the "hard work ethic are racist or sexist or were created by members of a particular race to oppress members of another race". [64]

The eight-member Oklahoma City Public Schools Board of Education, however, vehemently assailed the new

---

[64] Wallace, D. (2021, May 12). *Oklahoma City school board denounces new law banning critical race theory as protecting 'White fragility'.* Fox News. Retrieved May 12, 2021, from https://www.foxnews.com/us/oklahoma-city-school-board-critical-race-theory-white-fragility

legislation. One board member railed that the new act was an attempt to silence any discussions on race "in order to protect White fragility".[65]

The Governor of Oklahoma took issue with the claim that the new legislation was an attempt to silence discussions on race. He made it clear that it was important to teach history and past events in an honest manner. That includes such events as the Tulsa Race Massacre and the Trail of Tears. He emphasized that nothing in the legislation prevented or discouraged any conversations on those topics. He added that history can be taught without stigmatizing a child as an oppressor or making them feel guilty or shameful based upon their race or sex.[66]

Kudos to the state of Oklahoma for taking a position to prevent the indoctrination of its school children with critical race theory. Oklahoma, however, is not the only state that is trying to prohibit critical race theory from being taught in the classroom. As of May 2021, at least sixteen states have either

---

[65] Ibid.
[66] Ibid.

approved legislation or are considering bills that would limit

the teaching of certain concepts that are fundamental to critical

race theory.[67] Those states are: Arizona, Arkansas, Idaho,

Iowa, Louisiana, Mississippi, Missouri, New Hampshire, North

Carolina, Ohio, Oklahoma, Rhode Island, South Carolina,

Tennessee, Texas, and West Virginia.[68] Tennessee was the

most recent state on that list to approve legislation to ban the

teaching of critical race theory.

On June 10, 2021, the Florida State Board of Education

voted to ban the teaching of critical race theory in its public

schools.[69] Florida's Board of Education sought to prevent the

adoption of curriculum that would have had as its intended goal

the distortion of U.S. history. Not surprisingly, the supporters

of critical race theory opposed the ban. Their objective had

been to indoctrinate schoolchildren with racial propaganda and

---

[67] Associated Press. (2021, May 30). *State GOP lawmakers try to limit teaching about race, racism.* Fox News. Retrieved May 30, 2021, from https://www.foxnews.com/politics/state-gop-lawmakers-try-to-limit-teaching-about-race-racism

[68] Ibid.

[69] Calvan, B.C. (2021, June 10). *Florida bans 'critical race theory' from its classrooms.* AP. Retrieved June 10, 2021, from https://apnews.com/article/florida-race-and-ethnicity-government-and-politics-education-74d0af6c52c0009ec3fa3ee9955b0a8d

to replace the teaching of facts on the history of our nation with an anti-American agenda that would rewrite U.S. history based on the falsehood of systemic racism.

The advocates of critical race theory are like the nihilists who had followed the teachings of the nineteenth century German philosopher, Friedrich Nietzsche. The nihilists had no loyalties and did not believe in anything except a propensity for destruction. Nietzsche stated that nihilism came from the questioning of traditional values until they fell apart. He referred to that as "values destruction". The forces behind critical race theory have as their intention the destruction of American values by the rewriting of U.S. history and the brainwashing of American youth with socialist propaganda.

On the other hand, those in opposition to critical race theory have begun their fight to preserve and protect American values. That includes the education of their children. There is still a great deal to be done, however, in the battle to regain control over our schools. Whom will prevail in the battle for the soul of our nation's schools?

13. Just Say "No!"

During the summer of 2020, I had attended a community forum on racial justice organized by the Sheriff's Department in my county. Attendees were allowed to speak and voice any concerns they may have had on social justice. Additionally, suggestions were sought from participants on what steps could be taken to improve the relationship between the Sheriff's Department and residents of the county.

There was a young female (Crazy Daisy I will call her) who addressed the audience from the podium. She ranted about systemic racism and her White guilt. Crazy spoke in an emotional manner and scolded White people for their inaction to address racism in the U.S. Hearing Crazy Daisy speak was like listening to the confession of a sinner before a Catholic priest. With her voice trembling, she sought forgiveness for her "Whiteness" and the crimes committed against black people by the White race. Additionally, Craze implored the rest of us to do the same because of our alleged role in contributing to systemic racism. We were deemed guilty of racism solely for having been born a member of the White race. Sitting in a chair a few feet from the podium where she was standing, I softly and politely suggested, "Speak for yourself, madam."

Crazy Daisy left little doubt that she had been converted to the doctrine of critical race theory, which teaches that White people are born in sin, the sins of slavery and the genocide of indigenous people. Oprah Winfrey, the black personality on television, reaffirmed that doctrine, when she had chastised White America by having stated that we (Whites) have our whiteness, which affords us our "White privilege". Moreover, let's not forget the principal of a school in New York who had wanted to convert White parents into White abolitionists in a bizarre attempt to pressure them into denying their heritage and becoming messengers of their own obliteration. Furthermore, we need to empathize with the children at a middle school in California, who had been given an assignment, which asked them to comment on an opinion article titled, "Why I'm A Racist". Is there any doubt, that the assignment was intended to instill guilt into those children?

How does one respond to the advocates of critical race theory who insist that we must accept their perverted attempts to rewrite our nation's history and apologize for centuries of alleged "systemic racism"? Earlier I had written that during the 1980s, former First Lady Nancy Reagan, had adopted the battle cry, "Just Say No to Drugs" in her war on drugs campaign. In response to those who clamor that we must reshape our nation's history around the tenets of critical race theory, if I may paraphrase Mrs. Reagan, "Just say no to critical race theory".

Chapter Nine

Black Criminals White Victims

1. Figures Don't Lie but Liars Figure

The U.S. Department of Justice (DOJ) and the Federal

Bureau of Investigation (FBI) have provided statistics on

violent and non-violent crime in the U.S. They include arrests

that have been made based on the race and ethnicity of the

perpetrators. Unfortunately, those results are generally not

reported by the so-called mainstream media (MSM) in the U.S.

The MSM comprises news outlets such as CBS, NBC, ABC,

MSNBC, CNN, PBS, and NPR. In addition, it includes

publications such as The New York Times and The

Washington Post. The reason the MSM has failed to give

adequate coverage on crimes based on race is because, in doing

so, it will not advance its narrative. Its narrative is that blacks

have been victims of systemic racism and society needs to look

the other way when members of the black community commit

heinous crimes, especially those against the Caucasian

community.

According to the FBI's Uniform Crime Reporting (UCR) program, in 2017 there were 9,468 total arrests for murder and nonnegligent manslaughter in the U.S. Of that number, blacks and African Americans accounted for 5,025 of those crimes. On the other hand, Caucasians were responsible for 4,188 crimes.[70]

Based on those numbers, the black race had committed 53.07 percent of the murders and nonnegligent manslaughter crimes. Compare the percent of murders committed by blacks with their percent of the population in the U.S. We find that blacks made up approximately 13 percent of the U.S. population but committed 53 percent of the murders in the U.S. in 2017.

What the statistics tell us is that blacks commit violent crimes disproportionately in comparison to their racial counterparts. The mainstream media, however, continues to downplay that fact. In addition, the crimes committed by blacks against Whites are given scant coverage. That is also the

---

[70] FBI:UCR. (n.d.). *2017 Crime in the United States Table 43A*. FBI. Retrieved January 7, 2022, from https://ucr.fbi.gov/crime-in-the-u.s/2017/crime-in-the-u.s.-2017/tables/table-43

case for crimes committed by blacks against blacks and other

racial groups. Those crimes are accorded nothing more than a

footnote in news reports. The figures on black crime do not lie,

but the lying mainstream media believes that if it ignores those

facts, so will the rest of society.

2. The "Combat Zone"

Boston's notorious "Red-Light District" or "Combat

Zone" was aptly named for its reputation as an area for sex,

drugs, and death. Surprisingly, its location was not where one

might expect to find it in a large city. Facing south of the Zone

were the retail and financial districts. North of it were the

theatre district and one of Boston's celebrated hospitals, Tufts

Medical Center (Tufts-New England Medical Center until

2008). In addition, rubbing elbows with the Combat Zone was

Boston's "Chinatown". If a pedestrian wanted to walk from the

financial and retail districts to the Medical Center or to the

theater district, they would invariably have to pass through the

Combat Zone.

Commencing with the early evening hours up through the wee hours of the morning, however, the Combat Zone took on a life of its own. It was a predatory atmosphere. Hookers and their pimps preyed on a gullible public. Drug dealers sold their wares. Porn shops and strip clubs showcased their enticing assets. Moreover, robberies and murders were in abundance in the district.

Two of the most brutal murders that had ever occurred in the Zone were committed by black thugs against defenseless White victims. Do they come any other way?

We will call our first blood-soaked victim, Austin from Boston. His murder occurred when a taxi carrying him and a female companion had been stalled in traffic on a roadway running perpendicular to the Combat Zone. The female companion's husband, unable to accompany his wife that day, had asked his friend Austin to chaperone his wife. Austin agreed and by doing so sealed his fate.

Unable to proceed unobstructed to its destination, the taxi had exposed itself as a target to marauding gangs of felons. Two black thugs approached the taxi and ordered everybody out of the cab. They proceeded to rob the victims. Austin and his female companion had offered no resistance to the thugs and complied with their demands. One of the thugs, however, was not content with the money he had removed from Austin's wallet. Instead, he had decided to leave his calling card, which was to slit the throat of Austin. Blood poured relentlessly out of poor Austin's throat. He dropped to his knees on the roadway and cried out for help, but nobody came to his rescue. It should come as no surprise that no arrests were made by the Boston Police Department. Welcome to the Combat Zone!

Our next victim, call him Nick, was a male college student. He was knifed to death by a black pimp, whom I will call Leroy. It was the event that became the straw that broke the camel's back and led to the dismantling of the Combat Zone. Well, sort of, in a way.

The incident occurred when Nick and his male friends had decided to go into town for some entertainment in Boston's Red-Light District. Unfortunately for Nick, a black hooker picked his pocket and had stolen his wallet. Nick struggled to retrieve his wallet but was met with strong resistance from the hooker. Suddenly, her black pimp appeared out of the darkness and decided he would defend her from Nick's attempts to retrieve his stolen wallet. Leroy pulled out a combat knife and proceeded to slash poor Nick to death. This time the Boston Police were "Johnny-on-the-spot" and arrested the pimp. Leroy was charged with murder. At the trial, the pimp's attorney rambled on about how his client was simply protecting his employee from being attacked by Nick. The jury returned a guilty verdict, and the pimp was sentenced to twenty years in prison, with the potential for early release based on good behavior. The defense attorney approached Nick's family in the courtroom and offered his condolences on the loss of their son. Of course, he added how he was just doing his job and it was nothing personal. Yeah, maybe not personal for him, but it was personal for Nick's family.

That case marked the beginning of the end of Boston's notorious Red-Light District, the infamous Combat Zone. An infuriated public demanded a dismantling of the Zone. The hookers and pimps, for the most part, were driven out of the area. Additionally, many of the porn shops and strip clubs relocated to other areas. As you walk through the Combat Zone today, there are still remnants of the old days; however, it pales in comparison to what it was in its notorious heyday.

3. Mayhem in the Graveyard

In May 2020, an elderly White couple from Maryland were executed by a black male at a cemetery in Delaware. They had been paying their respects at the gravesite of their son. The couple, Paul and Lidia, were not a threat to their assailant. The black male ambushed them and without hesitation shot the couple stone cold dead. Paul, a U.S. Army veteran, and Lidia were in their mid-eighties. They had been married for over sixty years. [71]

The couple had visited their son's grave at Delaware Veterans' Cemetery practically every day, barring inclement weather, since his death in 2017. The gunman was identified as Sheldon, a black male in his late twenties. Police were not

---

[71] Calicchio, D. (2020, May 17). *Maryland couple slain at Delaware veterans cemetery visited son's grave almost daily, surviving son says.* Fox News. Retrieved May 17, 2020, from https://www.foxnews.com/us/maryland-couple-slain-at-delaware-veterans-cemetery-visited-sons-grave-almost-daily-surviving-son-says

aware of any apparent motive at the time of the murders. According to a news report, no confirmation was readily available, on whether the gunman committed suicide or was shot dead by police.[72]

The death of the couple was a hideous crime committed in the most cowardly manner. The assailant snuck up on the couple without apparent warning and executed them gangland style. Is there any doubt that this was a racially motivated crime? The national media reported on the murders in a cavalier manner, however, failing to address the killings as a possible hate crime.

4. Nursing Home Tragedy

It is a gut-wrenching experience for children to commit a parent into a nursing care facility. Moreover, parents usually feel as if their children have abandoned them and do not love them any more for having placed them in a nursing home. Without question, it is a stressful experience for all family members.

---

[72] Ibid.

In May 2020, a 75-year-old White male, Norman, was savagely beaten by a 20-year-old black male, Jayden, at Detroit's Westwood Nursing Center. According to reports, Norman had suffered four broken fingers, broken ribs, and a broken jaw. He died approximately two months after the severe beating. Family members claimed that the senior citizen had been depressed and not eating well since the vicious beating.[73]

Why was a 20-year-old black male a patient in a nursing care facility designed to care for senior members of our community? What happened to the assailant? Again, this is a case where the national media provided scant information to the public in the hopes that the crime will be forgotten by most Americans. The national media wants to perpetuate the lie that the U.S. is a racist nation. It fears that reporting on this type of news story would lead to a stigmatization of the black community. That would conflict with its agenda.

---

[73] Fox 2. (2020, July 27). *Elderly man allegedly beaten by 20-year-old at Detroit nursing home, dies.* Retrieved July 27, 2020, from https://www.fox2detroit.com/news/elderly-man-allegedly-beaten-by-20-year-old-at-detroit-nursing-home-dies

5. Five-Year-Old Shot Dead

In another violent act committed by a black male against a White victim, a 5-year-old child was shot dead while riding his bicycle outside his father's home. In August 2020, little Cannon was shot in the head in front of his two sisters, aged eight and seven. The assailant was identified as 25-year-old Darius, a black male, who was charged with first-degree murder. According to reports, a neighbor who had witnessed the shooting from her window, stated that Darius ran up to Cannon and put his gun to the little boy's head. He then shot him before turning around and running back into his own home.[74]

Media reports at the time of the shooting, stated that there was no motive that police could provide to explain the reason for such an abhorrent crime. Was this a racially motivated murder? Three months earlier, George Floyd, a notorious black felon, had died at the hands of a police officer

---

[74] WSOCTV News Staff. (2020, August 16). *'I screamed': Father of slain 5-year-old can't fathom why son was killed.* Retrieved August 16, 2020, from https://www.wsoctv.com/news/local/nc-man-accused-shooting-5-year-old-neighbor-head-point-blank-range/NLF2XRMIGRDVNNY67BI4KCICY4/

while resisting arrest in Minneapolis. The Floyd death

culminated in nationwide riots. Was this cowardly act

performed in retaliation for the death of Floyd? Unfortunately,

the national media was too preoccupied with the death of

George Floyd to commit its resources to investigate and report

on the execution-style murder of Cannon. Shame on the media!

God bless the family of Cannon!

6. Four-Year-Old Boy Abducted and Murdered

The brutal murder of Cash, a 4-year-old White male, in

Dallas, Texas in May 2021 shocked the senses of that

community. According to reports, home surveillance video had

recorded the abduction of the boy. The child had been asleep

when a man lifted him out of bed and carried him off from his

home. The victim's body, which had been lying in the street in

a pool of blood, was discovered by a jogger. According to

police, it appeared that the child suffered a violent death and

that an edged weapon had been used to inflict multiple stab

wounds on his body. The assailant was identified as Darriynn, an 18-year-old black male. He had been charged with capital murder.[75]

According to reports, three months earlier, Darriynn had been involved in another incident. In that case, he had allegedly entered a home without permission and had attempted to take the homeowner's infant granddaughter. In addition, reports stated, that when the granddad intervened, Darriynn had allegedly struck him in the head and had fled the home. The homeowner, however, did not want to press charges against Darriynn.[76] Had grandpa done so, would Cash be alive today? It appears that we will never know the answer to that question.

(Note: The murder of Cash is an ongoing case. As of this writing, there has been no trial. The accused is being held in jail. Moreover, it appears that the accused may also be

[75] Haney, A. and Rozier, A. (2021, May 28). *Suspect in case of 4-year-old found dead faces new charges*. WFAA. Retrieved May 28, 2021, from https://www.wfaa.com/article/news/local/new-charges-suspect-cash-gernon-case-separate-incident/287-6a10bf20-a00e-49c9-897e-fbc8f944886f

Fox News. (2021, May 17). *Video shows slain Dallas 4-year-old being taken from bed*. Retrieved May 17, 2021, from https://www.foxnews.com/us/video-shows-slain-dallas-4-year-old-being-taken-from-bed

[76] Ibid.

facing charges on the earlier incident involving the elderly

homeowner.)

7. Death at Dunkin' Donuts

According to the booking records at the Hillsborough

County Sheriff's Office in Florida, an employee at a Dunkin'

Donuts location was charged with aggravated manslaughter of

an elderly or disabled adult. What began as a verbal

disagreement between a customer and an employee at the

donut shop escalated into a physical encounter. A 27-year-old

black male, Corey, of Tampa was accused of throwing a punch

at a 77-year-old White male in May 2021. The elderly

gentleman was punched in the face, fell to the ground, and hit

his head on the concrete floor. Sadly, the injuries proved fatal

to the senior citizen.[77]

Corey, who was the manager on duty, claimed the

elderly gentlemen had used a racial slur which had provoked

---

[77] D'Angelo, B. (2021, May 11). *Dunkin' employee in Florida accused of fatally punching customer who used racial slur.* Action News Jax. Retrieved May 11, 2021, from https://www.actionnewsjax.com/news/trending/dunkin-employee-florida-accused-fatally-punching-customer-who-used-racial-slur/KGOQSXHV2VFL5JZQZC3VYE2SDA/

the altercation. According to State Attorney Andrew Warren, however, the charge of manslaughter was appropriate because the assailant punched the man without any legal justification resulting in his death. Moreover, Warren stated that although the racial slurs were inflammatory, they did not justify violence. The senior's speech was legal, according to Warren.[78]

In a bizarre turn of events, however, Corey was allowed to plead guilty to felony battery and was sentenced to two years of house arrest. The judge in the case also ordered him to complete 200 hours of community service. Additionally, he was instructed to attend a course on anger management.[79]

Wow!

---

[78] White, D. L. (2021, May 27). *Despite Racial Slur, Manslaughter Charge Upheld By State Attorney.* Patch. Retrieved May 27, 2021, from https://patch.com/florida/southtampa/despite-racial-slur-state-attorney-upholds-manslaughter-charge

[79] Associated Press. (2022, March 8*). Florida Dunkin' worker sentenced for fatal punch of customer.* Fox Business. Retrieved April 15, 2022. from https://www.foxbusiness.com/lifestyle/florida-dunkin-worker-sentenced-fatal-punch-customer

8. Macy's Beat Down

Macy's Department Store in Flint, Michigan was the scene of a brutal attack on one of its managers in June 2020. According to surveillance video, an 18-year-old black male customer, Damire, allegedly sucker punched the store's White manager, who had been working in the men's clothing section. It appeared that the provocateur approached the manager from behind, punched him in the head, and knocked him to the floor. While the manager was on the floor, the assailant continued to repeatedly strike the gentleman. Damire was charged with intent to do great bodily harm to the manager. [80]

Can you believe that Damire was sentenced to only two years of probation? Is that fair and just? Why wasn't he charged with a hate crime? Additionally, he allegedly was supposed to serve 180 days in the county jail on an unrelated case.

---

[80] Martindale, M. (2020, June 26). *Man Charged in Flint Twp. Attack on Macy's employee.* The Detroit News. Retrieved June 26, 2020, from
https://www.detroitnews.com/story/news/local/michigan/2020/06/26/man-charged-flint-twp-attack-macys-employee/3266368001/

9. Hail Caesar

Little Caesars Restaurant in Augusta, Georgia was the scene of a brutal beating administered by a black female upon a White lady. Emily, the 22-year-old White victim, was savagely beaten by Brittany, the 25-year-old black assailant. The assault occurred in May 2021. What makes this more tragic is that Emily was caring for a baby at the time of the incident. Brittany allegedly pulled a chair out from under Emily sending her down onto the floor. She then grabbed her by the hair and punched her repeatedly in the head. Brittany then dragged Emily out the front door by her hair and threw her on the ground. Apparently, that was not enough, as the assailant then stomped on the victim's head.[81]

Emily, her face bloodied, got up crying, "My baby!" She was left with a swollen face, the result of cuts to her face, head, and neck. Additionally, she sustained a black eye.[82]

---

[81] Aaro, D. (2021, May 19). *Georgia Little Caesars attack caught on video; woman wanted for battery.* Fox News. Retrieved May 19, 2021, from https://www.foxnews.com/us/georgia-woman-wanted-for-battery-in-attack-at-little-caesars-that-went-viral
[82] Ibid.

Fortunately, the baby whom the victim was caring for suffered no harm. Unfortunately, nobody tried to stop the beating.

10. Whitey in the Crosshairs

A multi-state shooting spree that resulted in five White males being shot and wounded by a black male was alleged to have been a racially motivated crime. According to the Columbus Police Department in Georgia, Justin Tyran Roberts was charged with shooting five people in three separate incidents in Georgia and Alabama. The shootings occurred in June 2021. Roberts had told police that he had been targeting White men. According to testimony by a detective with the Columbus Police Department, the 39-year-old Roberts had told him, "I had to have him", in reference to one of the shooting victims.[83]

Roberts was arrested on the following charges:

---

[83] Pagones, S. (2021, June 15). *Multi-state shooting spree was racially motivated, suspect was targeting White men: report.* Fox News. Retrieved June 15, 2021, from https://www.foxnews.com/us/racially-motived-gunman-targeting-white-men

- Aggravated Assault

- Possession of a Firearm During the Commission of a Crime

- Possession of a Firearm by a Convicted Felon

- Theft by Receiving Stolen Property (firearm)

  Additional warrants were to be obtained for:

- Aggravated Assault (3 counts)

- Possession of a Firearm during the Commission of a Crime

- Possession of a Firearm by a Convicted Felon

  (Per Columbus, Georgia Police Department's Facebook

Page)

According to the police department, Roberts middle name was Tyran. Would that be short for tyran(nosaurus), as in Tyrannosaurus Rex? Whether it is or not, Roberts certainly stirred enough commotion to rival that of ole Rex.

11. Granny Woke

There are Caucasians, especially White women, who have become guilt-ridden over what they believe to be the unfair treatment of people of color by our nation's justice system. In addition, they have a rather jaundiced view of our nation's history, especially as it pertains to black Americans. To cleanse themselves of ancestral guilt, for what they perceive to be the iniquities committed by White America against the black race, they blindly offer themselves as unwitting participants for the advocacy of black propaganda. It should come as no surprise then, that participation in activities such as Black Lives Matter protests, have become a form of catharsis for their imagined guilt.

The adage, "Be careful what you ask for, you just might get it", probably best describes the fate suffered by our victim, Granny Woke. Granny was a 75-year-old White woman who had retired from the Florida Department of Elder Affairs. She was described by those who knew her as an activist in Democrat politics. In addition, she allegedly had been a participant in Black Lives Matter (BLM) events. Furthermore, Granny allegedly had met a young black female activist, Jemimah, at one of the protests. Jemimah, all of 19-years-old, was described as an ardent BLM protester. Was this a match made in heaven or some such place? Given their fate, it was definitely not heaven.

So, what do you get when you mix a 75-year-old White grandma with a 19-year-old black female who was an outspoken advocate of black politics? You get trouble. Trouble, as in a 49-year-old black male, with a very long rap sheet, and a history of victimizing women. Let's call him Roscoe. It remains vague, however, what brought together all three protagonists. Call it fate.

According to law enforcement, both females were murdered by Roscoe. Moreover, the murders had taken place in the Tallahassee, Florida area in June 2020. Furthermore, Roscoe had confessed to killing both women. For his crimes, Roscoe was indicted on first-degree murder and other charges in the brutal slaying of both women.

It should be noted that fictitious names have been substituted for the actual names of the victims and their assailant. Additionally, I have referred to BLM events as protests and not riots. Many of those events, however, start out peacefully, but quickly unravel into a riot. Therefore, the BLM event attended by our victims may have started out as a protest but may have culminated into a riot.

One of the problems with obtaining information on black-on-White crimes, however, is that the media outlets have been withholding vital information from the public. The media downplays the crime. The reason it does that is because reporting on black criminals does not lend itself to the media's agenda. That agenda attempts to promote the falsehood that the black community has been victimized by systemic racism perpetrated by White nationalists or White supremacists. How could the media report horrific crimes committed by black thugs against White persons and simultaneously justify its portrayal of them as victims of society? It cannot, therefore, it trivializes black on White crimes. Furthermore, I would be remiss if I did not mention the fact that many criminal acts performed by black thugs are also committed against persons of color. Those crimes are also downplayed by the media.

Granny Woke was survived by two daughters and several grandchildren. She was a 75-year-old retired state employee from Florida. So, it begs the question, what was

259

Granny doing at a Black Lives Matter protest? Granny should

have heeded the adage, "Be careful what you ask for, you just

might get it".

12. Restaurant Face-Off

In 2018, the Democrat Congresswoman from

California, Maxine Waters, called on her followers to confront

Trump administration members and supporters whenever they

were seen in public. Consistent with her long history of

incendiary remarks, she urged them to "create a crowd" and

"harass them (Trump officials)".[84] Waters is most definitely a

provocateur.

Somebody must have been listening to the vitriol

gushing forth from her lips because several incidents have

occurred nationwide over the ensuing years at various

restaurants that appear to embrace her tactics. White patrons

eager to partake of a bit of food and drink have been harassed

---

[84] Ehrlich, J. (2018, June 25). *Maxine Waters encourages supporters to harass Trump administration officials*. CNN. Retrieved June 25, 2018, from https://www.cnn.com/2018/06/25/politics/maxine-waters-trump-officials/index.html

by black activists. Unfortunately, disgruntled Caucasians have often joined the marauding herds of malcontents.

In 2020, Black Lives Matter protesters harassed White diners at an outdoor dining area in Pittsburgh. One of the agitators stole a drink from a couple's table. Another disillusioned person was heard yelling, "Fuck the White people that built this system!"[85] There were no apparent arrests made by law enforcement.

An outdoor dining area in St. Petersburg, Florida was the scene of another restaurant encounter between a White couple and black protesters. Demonstrators had sat down at a table occupied by a White couple, male and female, who were having dinner. The female called 911 on her cellphone for assistance. According to a video posted by *Inside Edition* on YouTube on September 25, 2020, the caller was heard telling the 911 dispatcher:

---

[85] Feis, A. (2020, September 7). *Watch Black Lives Matter protesters harass Pittsburgh diners*. New York Post. Retrieved September 7, 2020, from https://nypost.com/2020/09/07/black-lives-matter-protesters-harass-pittsburgh-diners/

"There's a riot going down and they're threatening me. I'm trying to eat dinner and they're at our table and they're cussing and threatening me."

Again, as in Pittsburgh, there were no apparent arrests made by law enforcement. There is something seriously wrong with our judicial system, when a group of bullies representing Black Lives Matter and other factions can disrupt the lives of law-abiding citizens, whose only offending characteristic is that they were born of the White race. Instead of allowing those degenerates to operate with impunity, as they spread fear among the White population, they should have been arrested and charged with a hate crime.

Moreover, Congresswoman Maxine Waters and any other public official who advocate violence should be censured by Congress. Additionally, they should be removed from their respective committee assignments. Those persons need to be a voice of calm, not an advocate of violent acts.

13. High on Mushrooms, Short on Brains

Florida, undeniably, is a vacation magnet. Indeed, tourism is the number one industry in the state of Florida. A recent incident, however, may give tourists second thoughts on planning a vacation to Florida.

Dustin, a 21-year-old father and husband, was shot dead at a Miami Beach restaurant in August 2021. Dustin sacrificed his life, so that his one-year-old son could live his life. Dustin is the quintessential "hero dad".

As Dustin and his family were dining in the restaurant, a crazed gunman walked through the door wielding a gun. The gunman pointed his gun in a menacing manner at Dustin's one-year-old son. Instinctively, Dustin stood up placing himself between the gunman and the baby boy. A shot rang out and Dustin dropped to the ground. While on the ground, the assailant shot him multiple times.

The suspected gunman was identified as Tamarius, a 22-year-old black male from Norcross, Georgia. Immediately after the shooting, Tamarius was caught on video dancing while patrons were heard screaming in the restaurant. The suspected killer, in panic mode, fled the restaurant on foot. He was captured by authorities a short distance from the establishment hiding in an alley. Tamarius allegedly told law enforcement that he had shot Dustin because he "was high on mushrooms, which made him feel empowered."[86] As of the writing of this book, he has been charged with murder and is confined to a cell while awaiting justice.

14. Reeducation of White Women

It began as a harmless walk in New York City's Central Park in the spring of 2020 but culminated in a verbal altercation between a black male and a White woman. If this incident had been a boxing match, the headline would have read, "Cooper vs. Cooper". The parties to the confrontation, however, were not related to one another.

Ms. Cooper had dialed 911 to request the help of law enforcement but ended up being charged with "filing a false

---

[86] Betz, Bradford. (2021, August 25). *Florida tourist shot dead while protecting his baby at Miami Beach restaurant.* Fox News. Retrieved October 19, 2021, from https://www.foxnews.com/us/florida-tourist-shot-dead-protecting-baby-miami-beach-restaurant

police report". The Manhattan District Attorney, Cy Vance Jr., described her actions as "racist".[87]

In lieu of facing charges over the incident, the defendant opted to accept an "alternative restorative justice solution". The so-called solution consisted of five therapy sessions of "psychoeducation and therapy services".[88] In addition, Ms. Cooper had been fired from her job at an investment firm.

There are many White women that I know who would not hesitate to call 911 for assistance, if they were accosted by a black male while taking a walk in a public park. Would that make those women racist? Indeed, women of any color may feel that their safety was being threatened if approached by an uninvited black male while walking in a park.

Several years ago, a study was performed that measured the reaction of test subjects to the presence of black males. The

[87] Wallace, D. and Dhanis, M. (2021, February 16). *NYC judge drops charges against Amy Cooper, woman in Central Park bird-watcher incident.* Fox News. Retrieved January 8, 2022, from https://www.foxnews.com/us/new-york-woman-central-park-black-birdwatcher-charges-dismissed-amy-cooper
[88] Ibid.

focus group was comprised of persons of various race and ethnic backgrounds. It included both male and female participants.

The subjects had electrodes attached to their bodies which measured their heart rate, respiration, and blood pressure. In addition, the test subjects were not apprised of the objective of the study.

As the participants sat in the room, males comprising Caucasian, Asian, and African American backgrounds entered the room one at a time. The results of the study revealed that when a black male had entered the room, the subjects' vital signs had increased to varying degrees. When an Asian or Caucasian male had entered the room, however, the vital signs of the participants remained relatively stable. The test results were consistent irrespective of the racial, ethnic background, and gender of the participants.

In general, the study's report had concluded that the vital signs of the test subjects had become elevated when a black male had appeared before the group. The study, however, did not examine the reason for the participants' reactions and therefore offered no conclusion on that matter.

The results of the study were a revelation. Based on the study's findings, I believe that we can fairly state, that there is a genuine fear (or apprehensive uneasiness) of black males, albeit to varying degrees, among the general population.

Why was it then, that a White woman who had called 911 after being accosted by a black male in the park, had to suffer the loss of her job, the stigmatization of her character, and the humiliation of having to attend five therapy sessions? That is not justice.

15. Better to be Judged by Twelve Than Carried by Six

Given that there is a genuine anxiety among many individuals when they have a sudden encounter with black males, is it possible for those persons to overcome their phobia? The answer is yes.

In the early to mid-twentieth century, it was a common practice that tenants paid their rent to their landlord in cash.

Checking accounts were not widely in use by the general population, especially among the low to middle-income population at that time. In addition, credit cards were not widely prevalent as a form of payment. The landlord, or someone hired by the landlord, would generally visit the tenant, and collect the rent. Alternatively, the tenant could simply visit the landlord's office and pay the rent.

One summer's day in 1958, Grandpa John asked me if I would like to travel with him to Rhode Island's capital city, Providence, where he had to collect the rents for his employer, an inner-city landlord. It seemed that the landlord, a Jewish man, had a number of properties in the city with which he had been having problems collecting rents. The previous persons he had hired to collect the rents were greeted with hostility from several of the tenants. Those hostile actions included severe physical beatings. It had reached the point where nobody had wanted the job of collecting rents in a ghetto area. Consequently, many tenants were in arrears with their rents.

Grandpa John, although retired, was a former police officer. His brother, Leo, was a police Captain. Leo had won acclaim for his actions in apprehending a criminal while on vacation in New York City. According to news reports, he came upon police units that had an armed suspect cornered in an alley. Leo introduced himself and asked if he could be of service. New York's finest agreed to his offer. Leo walked into that alley, Dirty Harry style, disarmed the suspect, and knocked him out cold with one punch. That earns you nationwide celebrity status.

Given the reputation of both John and Leo, it was not surprising that Grandpa John was asked by the landlord if he would be willing to collect the rents on his properties. If anybody was going to have success in that role, it was going to be John.

In the 1950s, it was an adventuresome experience to visit the "big city". So, when Grandpa John asked me if I would accompany him to Providence on the day he was collecting rents, I didn't hesitate and had agreed to make the trip. When John and I had arrived in the city, we parked on Charles Street, which was your typical crime infested neighborhood in the 1950s. The area was rife with poverty, violence and predominantly black.

As I had exited the vehicle and firmly placed my feet on the pavement, a young black male approached me, pulled out a formidable looking knife, and yelled, "I am going to carve up your White ass". That threat froze me in my steps. On the other hand, John who had exited on the driver's side, looked over at the knife-wielding youth and dismissively declared, "Ignore him. We've got work to do." The black youth, to my relief, put away his knife. John and I then hurried across the street to a men's bar.

As we entered the pub, John cautioned me to remain at the entrance while he went to speak to one of the tenants. My eyes surveyed the layout of the club and noticed that all its patrons were black males. Those guys looked like some of the characters from the bar scene in the first Star Wars film. It was then that my life, short though it had been, flashed before my eyes. I remember thinking, "I am going to die here today. We (John and I) will both be killed."

John made his way over to the bar to speak to the tenant. He walked over in a nonchalant manner exuding the utmost confidence. He reminded me of John Wayne from one of Wayne's westerns. Grandpa John concluded his business with the tenant, and we walked out of the pub. He reminded me that there were rents that still had to be collected before we went home. The rest of the afternoon consisted of visiting tenants and collecting the rents that were due for the week. With the conclusion of our business, we bid farewell to the ghetto and returned home.

In retrospect, the participation in that day's events provided me with a life-learning experience that added to my personal growth and maturity. Surviving the knife-wielding thug, the bar scene, and meeting several of the tenants helped to dispel any apprehensions that I may have had about encounters with members of the black race. Thankfully, that proved to be a benefit which unquestionably contributed to my well-being and survival in future years from close encounters with members of the black race.

One event that I had been fortunate to survive occurred in the spring of 1991. I had been attending a birthday bash being held for a friend at an upscale restaurant. As darkness had fallen, I had left the festivities and walked out of the restaurant to the rear of the building where I had parked my vehicle. Proceeding cautiously in the poorly lit area, I made my way along the uneven pavement that was littered with debris. The neighborhood was under demolition as part of an urban renewal effort to renovate the downtown area. As I was about to enter my auto, however, a black male approached me in the darkness. He was dressed in a dark coat with a dark ski hat pulled over his dark head. He placed his hand on my shoulder and demanded that I give him money. That was a mistake. Instinctively, I uttered some choice words, while I simultaneously removed his hand with one arm and flipped him over onto the pavement with my other arm. Astonished, he picked himself up off the pavement, laughed nervously, and scurried away.

The next day I had visited the central police station that was located in the downtown area to file a report of the incident. The reason for filing a report was to alert the police of a potential threat to law-abiding citizens who may visit the same area in the future. The desk sergeant at the station told me that I had been extremely fortunate that I had escaped with no injuries. He added that a person had been murdered in the same area two weeks earlier. Moreover, he commended me for my quick reaction which most likely took the thug by surprise and caused him to run off into the night like a terrified fox being pursued by hounds.

When I had asked the police sergeant if he had any photos that I could look at to identify the suspect, he said that he did but that it would be a waste of my time. I implored incredulously, "Why would it be a waste of time?"

He replied, "Even if you could identify him in a photo, I would then have to place him in a lineup from which you would need to identify him again. A bunch of black males all wearing ski hats in a lineup? Forget it! But if you insist, you can try; however, it will be a waste of your time."

At that point, I had decided not to continue my pursuit of the issue. Notwithstanding the reluctance of the sergeant, I had one final question of him and that was, "What can I do in the future to protect myself from being robbed or murdered if the police are not there to provide assistance." He replied, "Carry a gun."

Truly, I believe that by showing no fear to the black assailant, I was able to catch him off guard and had survived a potential disaster. Moreover, at that time, cellphones were not in widespread usage. Therefore, I could not have called 911 for assistance. My advice to the public is that if you find yourself in a confrontation with a thug, do not display any fear for it may be taken as a sign of weakness and expose you to imminent harm. Furthermore, call 911. Make the call! Ignore the so-called "Karen laws" that make it a crime to summon the police about a threatening black male. Remember, this is your life that is on the line.

Additionally, if you don't own a firearm, then purchase one for your protection. Learn how to use it in a safe manner and only fire it at someone in self-defense to avoid your imminent death. Remember, it is better to be judged by twelve, than to be carried by six.

16. How the Failure to Call 911 Led to a Young Woman's Death

In 2020, the Board of Supervisors in San Francisco

approved legislation known as the "Caren Act" which made it a

hate crime to call 911 on people of color.[89] It was a knee-jerk

reaction to the death of George Floyd, a notorious black felon,

at the hands of the Minneapolis police.

The "Caren Act" exploited the nomenclature "Karen",

which had been appropriated by Black Lives Matter supporters

to describe White women who call the police over their

apprehensiveness regarding people of color, especially black

males. The legislation would give people of color the legal

authority to sue 911 callers in civil court. In addition, the

Governor of California approved legislation making such

actions a punishable crime.[90] Not to be upstaged by California,

---

[89] Associated Press. (2020, October 20). *San Francisco's 'Caren Act' makes placing racist 911 calls a hate crime.* The Guardian. Retrieved January 22, 2022, from https://www.theguardian.com/us-news/2020/oct/20/caren-act-san-francisco-racist-911-calls

[90] Walker, T. (2020, October 1). *Governor Newsom Signs And Vetoes Closely Watched Criminal Justice Bills.* Witness LA. Retrieved January 22, 2022, from https://witnessla.com/governor-newsom-signs-and-vetoes-closely-watched-criminal-justice-bills/

other areas in the U.S. have begun to enact so-called "Karen" laws. New York, for example, approved a measure that would allow the offended person the right to sue the 911 caller.

Have the "Karen" laws succeeded in deterring 911 callers? You be the judge.

In January 2022, Los Angeles was the scene of a brutal slaying of a 24-year-old UCLA graduate student. The heinous crime had shaken the sensibilities of the city and the nation. The victim was Brianna, a White woman. She had been allegedly stabbed to death by a black male while she had been working at a furniture store. The alleged assailant was charged with murder and was being held on 2 million dollar bail.[91]

According to police, a customer found Brianna dead and lying on the floor in a pool of blood. The alleged assailant was a career criminal and had a long rap sheet from the east coast to the west coast. Additionally, police reported that

---

[91] Casiano, L., Ruiz, M., and Rosenberg, R. (2022, January 21). *Brianna Kupfer's alleged killer charged with murder in LA court.* Fox News. Retrieved January 22, 2022, from https://www.foxnews.com/us/brianna-kupfers-killer-murder-la-court

Brianna had texted her friend that a man was in the store and had made her feel uncomfortable.[92]

So why didn't Brianna call 911 and report the intruder? Did she hesitate because she did not want to be accused of a hate crime by calling 911? We will never know the answer.

It is time, however, to abolish the so-called "Karen" laws. Until those laws have been repealed, any woman, White or otherwise, should not hesitate to call 911 if she feels threatened by a stranger. Indeed, it is a matter of life and death.

17. The Sad Case of George Floyd

September 11, 2001 will be a day that will live forever in infamy in the history of our nation. That is the day on which we had witnessed attacks on U.S. soil by Islamic extremists. Thousands perished in the attacks which forever changed our way of life. The morning began when four planes were hijacked by Mideast terrorists. Two of those planes crashed into the World Trade Center in New York City killing approximately 3,000 people. Another plane struck the

---

[92] Ibid.

Pentagon building in Washington, D.C. A fourth plane was

thwarted from reaching the White House by passengers and

crew aboard the aircraft who had courageously wrestled control

of the plane from the hijackers. The plane, however, crashed

into a field in Pennsylvania killing all on board.

Our national leaders, fearful of future attacks by foreign

extremists, decided to implement draconian measures which

would allegedly protect us from threats by terrorists. Those

measures, however, would also restrict the rights of American

citizens by invading our privacy and by placing burdens on our

ability to travel. The tradeoff was "more security in exchange

for less privacy". To that end, the Department of Homeland

Security (DHS) and the Transportation Security Administration

(TSA) were created which allowed our government to monitor

our daily activities. Those "watchdog" agencies were given

broad powers over us, including but not limited to, financial

transactions, emails, telephone conversations, and travel

arrangements. In addition, law enforcement agencies were

given expanded police powers, presumably to protect us and

ensure our safety.

Unfortunately, one of the unintended outcomes of this government overreach was that American citizens were now being viewed as potential enemy combatants rather than as "neighbors-next-door". Everybody was a suspect. Police officers were allowed to shoot first and ask questions later. According to court rulings, law enforcement officers were given authority to shoot whomever they believed to be a perceived threat. And they could do so without consequences. Moreover, once the police began to shoot, they could continue shooting the suspect until he no longer posed a threat. As incomprehensible as it may seem, there were cases in which the bodies of suspects had been riddled with dozens of rounds of bullets. In one case, it was reported that up to 145 rounds of ammunition were fired at a suspect.

Unfortunately, the quick trigger decisions by some law enforcement officers, have led to the deaths of law-abiding citizens. In one incident, police were called to a nursing home to assist its staff with a patient who had been unwilling to comply with the staff's orders. It ended badly when the patient, a White male in his nineties, was fatally shot by an officer who had mistaken the spoon in the patient's hand for a weapon. If the officer had just used a little common sense, this tragedy could have been avoided and the old-timer may have simply died a natural death.

In another incident, a family member of a bed-ridden 106-year-old White male had called police because the elderly gentlemen had a gun in his possession while in bed and had refused to surrender the weapon. An entire SWAT team was sent to the residence and when the centenarian would not surrender his weapon to the SWAT team, he was unceremoniously shot to pieces in his own bed. Why couldn't the family member or SWAT team have exercised a little patience and allowed the elderly gentleman to eventually fall asleep? Then they could have entered his room and removed the firearm without incident.

Moreover, the expansion of government authority manifests itself in the way TSA employees have been given power to search and detain passengers with impunity at the airport. In the first year of operation of the TSA, several dozen passengers had died because of having been tasered by a TSA employee. Those passengers were not criminals but law-abiding citizens who had objected to bodily searches and the rummaging of their personal belongings by TSA personnel. The moral to those TSA confrontations is to never pin a badge on an employee with a low IQ.

The events which I have cited that had led to the deaths of two elderly men, one in the nursing home and the other one in his bed, were avoidable tragedies. Similarly, the deaths of those travelers who had been tasered at the airport were a tragic loss. In all instances, the deceased parties had been law-abiding citizens.

The "one size fits all" approach to the use of law-enforcement tactics ignores the fact that there is a difference between the good guys and the bad guys. Being able to distinguish between the two could save lives in the future.

What about hardened criminals? How should law enforcement deal with those individuals? The adage, "You reap what you sow", comes to mind. Law enforcement officers should not have their hands tied when it comes to dealing with convicted felons. Which brings us to the sad case of George Floyd.

George Floyd, a convicted black felon, died in May 2020 at the hands of a police officer in Minneapolis, Minnesota. The police had been called by an employee of a local business who had reported that Floyd had allegedly given him a counterfeit $20 bill. When police had arrived to arrest Floyd, he had become uncooperative and combative with the officers. Backup was summoned and additional police officers arrived at the scene. Floyd was still uncooperative and refused to be placed in a police cruiser. One of the officers, Derek Chauvin, had placed Floyd on the ground and held him there with his knee placed on Floyd's neck until he stopped resisting the officer. By that time, Floyd was lying motionless on the ground. He was later pronounced dead by medical personnel.

George Floyd had previously resided in Texas and had a very lengthy record of criminal activity. One of his most heinous crimes had occurred in 2007 when he was charged by the State of Texas with aggravated robbery while in possession of a deadly weapon. The following paragraphs describe the chain of events which led to the arrest of Floyd:

Aracely Henriquez was at her Houston home with her children when a man knocked on her door claiming to be from the water company. When she opened it, several men pushed her inside the home at gunpoint and pinned her on the couch.

"Where are the drugs? Where is the money?" Henriquez recalled the men screaming as they ransacked her kitchen cabinets, children's closets and drawers. The men pistol-whipped Henriquez before realizing they had the wrong house and ran out as quickly as they came in. Neighbors jotted down the license plate number of the getaway vehicle and passed it to police.

Henriquez said she could recall bits and pieces of the assailants' faces in the chaos. The man who stood out most was the "big guy," she said.

Three months later, Houston Police stopped the suspect vehicle and found Floyd — who stood 6 foot 6 — behind the wheel. It wasn't his car, but he was arrested, indicted on aggravated robbery charges and faced up to 40 years in prison. Investigators

brought photocopies of Floyd's mug shot as a photo

array to Henriquez to identify the man who put a gun

to her abdomen.

"I don't think I could forget that face," she said in an

interview with The Post.

In the report, police note that Henriquez "tentatively"

identified Floyd in a photo array. It was her 7-year-

old son — whose eyes were bathed in tears at the

time of the robbery, his mother said — who

positively identified Floyd by pointing him out in a

spread of photos. [93]

According to the criminal complaint issued by the State

of Texas, which was prepared on November 27, 2007, charging

George Floyd with aggravated robbery:

"....... Complainant Henriquez tentatively identified

Defendant George Floyd as being the largest of the

suspects who initially forced his way into her home,

pulled the pistol into her abdominal area, and forced

---

[93] Hernandez, Arelis R. (2020, October 26). *A knee on his neck.* The Washington Post. Retrieved October 19, 2021, from https://www.washingtonpost.com/graphics/2020/national/george-floyd-america/policing/

her into the living room area. Complainant Negrete

positively identified Defendant Floyd as being one of

the suspects whom he remembered seeing going

through the cabinets in the kitchen."

Floyd was offered a plea deal of five years in prison

which he quickly accepted, rather than face a jury trial that

could have ended up adding more years to his prison term. Do

you think this guy would have learned his lesson and have tried

to turn around his life?

A six foot six black male putting a gun to the abdomen

of a woman during a home invasion has to be a frightening

experience. Can you even begin to imagine the terror that lady

was put through by George Floyd and his posse? There are

unverified reports on the internet that the lady who had the gun

placed against her abdomen was pregnant. Pregnant or not

pregnant, that was a horrible act committed by George Floyd.

George Floyd, however, has become a martyr of sorts

to Black Lives Matter, ANTIFA, radical journalists, advocates

of critical race theory, and others who wish to tear down our

nation by subverting our culture. Personally, I believe that the radical elements have chosen the wrong poster boy for their idolization.

It is rather hyperbolic to describe Floyd in terms of a martyr, but he is unfortunately portrayed that way by radical elements of society. If the reader doubts my claim, then read what the Rev. Terrance W. Klein, a priest of the Diocese of Dodge City, had written about Floyd. Rev. Klein penned an article for America Magazine, titled "George Floyd died crying out to his mother. So did Jesus." [94]

How does a Catholic priest have the audacity to compare George Floyd with Jesus Christ? It is sheer blasphemy! Moreover, no mention of Floyd's criminal past was reported by Klein in his article. In the name of common decency, the Catholic Church should consider defrocking Klein.

During the period 2020-2021, the removal of statues and monuments of leaders from our nation's past has shaken

---

[94] Klein, Terrance. (2020, December 16). *George Floyd died crying out to his mother. So did Jesus.* America. Retrieved October 19, 2021, from https://www.americamagazine.org/faith/2020/12/16/george-floyd-jesus-scripture-advent-mother-reflection-239531

the foundation of the Republic. It has also cast a pall over our heritage. Replacing those artistic works with statues and busts of George Floyd is a revulsion to the moral conscience of law-abiding Americans. Our Founding Fathers are rolling over in their graves.

Radical elements are attempting to reshape the U.S. in the image of counter-culture heroes such as George Floyd. Is that the kind of person we want to elevate to the status of role model for our youth? What was Floyd's defining contribution to society? Placing a gun to the belly of a woman?

George Floyd met his destiny at the hands of the Minneapolis police. This is a case where the police exercised patience and restraint in attempting to arrest a felonious drug-fueled six foot six thug. Moreover, Floyd was a major contributing factor in his death. Sorry reader, but I find it difficult to feel empathy for a person who would put a gun to the belly of a woman.

Chapter Ten

At a Crossroads: The Future of Education

The future of education is at a crossroads. It is faced with the proverbial "fork in the road" dilemma. In all likelihood, the direction it chooses to take will profoundly affect countless generations of Americans.

One path will lead to the utter destruction of our institutions of learning. That road is fraught with hate, divisiveness, and ignores our core values. It embraces critical race theory and the rewriting of our nation's history.

There is another path, however, that will lead us to a revival of our traditional values. It promotes healing and unity. Additionally, it encourages each individual student to pursue programs of study that will enable them to become successful in their chosen careers. Moreover, it prepares our leaders of tomorrow to continue the work of our forefathers in building a better nation.

Earlier, I had discussed changes in the promotion-retention policies of our nation's public schools from its inception to the present day. The adoption of a "social promotion" policy signaled the end of having older adolescents in grade school alongside their much younger peers. Social promotions, however, had unintended consequences that proved to be as devastating as the policy of retaining older students in classrooms along with younger children. It led to students graduating from high school unable to read, write, and perform math at a satisfactory level.

To overcome the failed policy of handing out social promotions to students who did not possess basic skills, a new era in education was ushered in that promised "no child left behind". How did that work out in the education of our youth? No child left behind did create a number of new positions within our schools which were financed on the backs of tax-weary homeowners, but it had the effect of producing marginal results. Thus, young men and women continued to "graduate" from high school with minimal skills.

The state of Oregon has seemingly found a new way in which to give students a false sense of achievement upon graduation from high school. According to the educational brain trust in Oregon, they have concluded, "if a student cannot rise to our level of standards, then we must lower our standards to their level." That reminds me of a line from the story of Muhammad, which is, "If the mountain will not come to Muhammad, then Muhammad must go to the mountain." In Oregon, the prime beneficiaries of the lowering of standards to graduate from high school are minority students. It is Oregon's version of equitable education.

The state's new policy of lower graduation standards has been officially codified into Oregon law. The Governor of Oregon, Kate Brown, signed a bill that would suspend the requirement that high school graduates demonstrate an ability to read, write, and perform math at a high school level. A spokesperson for the governor explained that the new law would benefit "Oregon's Black, Latino, Latina, Latinx,

Indigenous, Asian, Pacific Islander, Tribal, and students of color."[95]

That brings us to the "duck test". The duck test can be described as a form of abductive reasoning. Here is its usual expression with which readers are most familiar: "If it looks like a duck, swims like a duck, and quacks like a duck, then it probably is a duck". Oregon's Board of Education, its governor, and its legislative branch can spin its new law every which way they please, but they cannot fool the public. A duck is a duck no matter how one camouflages it. Similarly, Oregon's new law is just another failed attempt to resolve the issue of student promotion and retention regardless of how the state promotes its new legislation. The new law fosters a false sense of achievement in students who have failed to demonstrate a satisfactory skillset upon graduation from high school. Additionally, it discriminates against the best and brightest minds.

---

[95] Hess, F. M. (2021, August 12). *Oregon Democrats Resurrect the 'Soft Bigotry of Low Expectations'*. The Dispatch. Retrieved October 19, 2021, from https://thedispatch.com/p/oregon-democrats-resurrect-the-soft

As the assault on our national heritage and nation's history continues unabatedly, the malignancy has spread to virtually all our institutions. These institutions include, but are not limited to, education, military branches of service, advertising, government agencies, fraternal organizations, the film industry, the arts, business enterprises, banking, news agencies, social media, and sports. In effect, our institutions have now become factories for social justice.

The National Football League (NFL) is one example of an institution that has been in the forefront of the assault on our national culture and a strong proponent of critical race theory. The NFL, in its infinite and twisted wisdom, had mandated the playing of two anthems prior to kickoff of its scheduled games during the 2021-2022 season.

Notwithstanding the fact that there is only one National Anthem, "The Star-Spangled Banner", the league has adopted the song, "Lift Every Voice and Sing", as another anthem to be played before games. The song is considered the "black national anthem" among its supporters. Supporters include the black community, proponents of critical race theory, and those who are working assiduously to cancel our national culture.

There are three primary attributes which define us as a nation. They are borders, language, and culture. Without borders to secure our safety, without a common language with which to conduct our daily lives, and without a common shared culture that defines us as a people, we could not claim nationhood status. Only one national anthem, "The Star-Spangled Banner", reflects those attributes. It defines us as a people and unites us as a nation.

A black national anthem would be appropriate if the U.S. was a black nation. It would also be appropriate if the NFL was a professional sports league in Africa. The U.S., however, is not a black nation and the NFL is not a professional sports league in Africa.

A black national anthem will only serve to divide us as a people. It will not unite us as one people. On the other hand, "The Star-Spangled Banner" is all inclusive. It represents all persons within our nation.

What has taken place in the NFL is a microcosm of what is happening throughout our great land. Moreover, there is a trickle-down effect from institutions like the NFL to universities and even to our public schools. Colleges, especially black colleges, play the so-called black national anthem before their games and campus ceremonies. Furthermore, many universities have different graduation ceremonies for black and White students. It is not uncommon for universities to hold graduation events for Latino, Black, Native, Asian, LGBTQ, first-generation graduating, and low-income students in addition to the main graduating ceremony. Columbia University acknowledged this when it issued the following statement:

"The smaller celebratory events held for particular communities are in addition to, not instead of, the main Commencement and Class Day graduation ceremonies."[96]

Other colleges in the U.S., including Georgetown, Yale, and Princeton have held similar multicultural graduation

---

[96] Lajka, A. (2021, March 16). *Columbia University holds a main graduation, as well as smaller ceremonies.* AP. Retrieved October 19, 2021, from https://apnews.com/article/fact-checking-afs:Content:9987564288

events. Additionally, at the public school level, children have become hyper-aware of race and are unwittingly being set into conflict with each other based on the color of their skin.

Standing at the crossroads of the future of education, do we continue along a precipitous path that will take us to the eve of destruction? Or do we follow the road that will lead us to the salvation and renewal of our educational system?

The good news is that Americans have begun to strike back against the proponents of critical race theory and the thugs that comprise Black Lives Matter. Opposition is evident

Illustration courtesy of Robert V. Carabina.

throughout our nation.

In Oklahoma, the governor signed into law a bill that forbids the teaching of the underlying concepts of critical race theory. Moreover, Florida's State Board of Education has voted to ban outright the teaching of critical race theory in its public schools. Additionally, parents and teachers in Virginia, as well as elsewhere, have expressed their opposition to critical race theory at tempestuous school board meetings.

The road to victory is never easy. It is fraught, unfortunately, with perilous obstacles. In the case of our public schools, those obstacles threaten the foundation of our educational system. With the continued involvement of concerned parents, teachers, and political leaders, however, our educational system can once again become a paradigm of learning excellence. To paraphrase the Welsh poet Dylan Thomas,

"We will not go gentle,

without a good fight."